Spirits of the
Salmon River

BACKEDDY

Backeddy Books
Cambridge, Idaho 83610
208/257-3810

Design:
W. Roger Cole, Cole + Company, Inc.; Boise, Idaho

ISBN 0-9710813-0-1

Spirits of the
Salmon River

Kathy Deinhardt Hill

Introduction

The truth depends on who you ask. While we all like to think the history we read is accurate, accuracy is as ephemeral as time itself. History is a collection of eyewitness accounts; however, no two persons remember events in the same way. Add the secondhand recollections and fading memories, and fact and fiction become intertwined. It is then written down and passed on as truth.

In *Spirits of the Salmon River,* I intended to produce an accurate history of the people who are buried alongside the river. Using previously published sources, oral histories, newspapers, county archives, and military and census records, I did my best to record their stories as I found them.

While the entry for each individual is as accurate as I could confirm, the book does not include everyone who died and is buried on the river. With the gold rush in the late 1800s and the land rush in the early 1900s, thousands of now nameless persons wandered the Salmon River corridor searching for a better life. How many of them lost their lives in the search and were buried on the river cannot now be known. Over the past three years, I was told countless stories of gravesites, but without names or dates they truly became the spirits of the Salmon River.

Inclusion of the gravesite photographs testifies to the lives of the persons we do know. Of course, we have their stories, but the graves make the stories real. I have included information on where to find each grave. Some are in established cemeteries and protected by caretakers; others are in neglected areas, often on the banks of the river. In these instances, I give a general description. The truly curious, who love Idaho and its history, will seek them out. I hope that anyone who happens upon these graves will accord them the respect they deserve.

Many people contributed to my efforts. Most important are Jim and Mary Lou Rush and Richard Waite. They were with me every step as we searched the banks of the Salmon River. This book would not have been possible without their help. Others who were instrumental are Clay Morgan, whose enthusiasm inspired me to start the project; Rick Ardinger and the Idaho Humanities Council, whose grant allowed me to travel the state with my photos and stories; and Earl Brockman, whose work in the darkroom was invaluable.

Finally, I am forever grateful to my husband Bob, whose encouragement and support guided me through every rapid on this wonderful three-year journey.

Kathy Deinhardt Hill

Foreword

The Salmon River winds its way through the heart of Idaho; its cliffs, violent waters, and narrow passageways discouraged early explorers, even Captain William Clark. But this turbulent river with all of its dangers became an artery for many who flocked to it. They and the river merged as they carved their lives within its canyons and on its bars.

The migration to the Salmon River began with the discovery of gold in the Florence Basin in 1861. By 1862 approximately 10,000 people swarmed the area, establishing towns in Warren, Elk City, and Dixie. From the south, miners fanned out from the Boise Basin diggings to the Salmon River and its tributaries, creating mining towns in Leesburg, Bonanza, and Shoup, among others. Today mining operations can still be found along the river's banks.

While the lure of gold called many, free land and a fresh start brought others. The mild climate allowed hard-working people a chance to succeed. The rugged trails, heavy mountain snows, and high spring runoff guaranteed that visitors would be discouraged; those who chose to live on the Salmon River could do so in relative obscurity. They were trappers, hunters, ranchers, farmers, outlaws. The Salmon River became their home. It fed them and captivated them and they became a part of it. It became the place where they would live and die.

The river took many of them, sweeping them away in its swollen spring currents, pulling them down, never to be seen again. As the *Idaho County Free Press* reported in May of 1902, "Several dead bodies have been seen floating down the Salmon. Since no one has been reported missing, it's unlikely we'll discover who these poor people are."

Harsh, frozen winters claimed others, as did treacherous trails. From rattlesnakes to ruffians, early settlers on the Salmon faced danger at every turn, and many of them died alone. If they were lucky enough to be found, they were buried quickly, more often in unmarked graves, and then forgotten.

But there were those who by circumstance or design left an indelible impression, whose spirits echo through the canyon where they spent their last days. They are unforgettable characters whose triumphs and tragedies have become a part of our history, like the river itself.

From North Fork down to Whitebird, these are their stories.

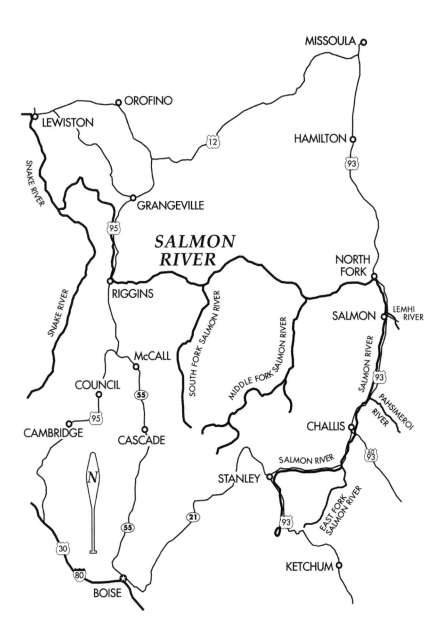

Solomon Parks

In the 1800s, many men left their homes in search of their fortunes. Solomon Parks searched much farther than most. Although he died a broken old man on the banks of the Salmon River, Parks had filled his life with adventure.

Parks was born January 13, 1822, in Burton, Ohio. He was the son of Warham Parks and Sally Edson Parks. Having moved west from Maryland, Solomon's father, uncle, and grandfather were pioneer settlers of Geauga County.

Solomon Parks is buried in a small cemetery at the Indianola Ranger Station, 10.4 miles west of North Fork, Idaho on the Salmon River Road. It is located on a small hill approximately 100 yards north of the ranger station. Parks' grave is located in the northeast corner of the cemetery.

Solomon's grandfather, Nathan Parks, was a veteran of the Revolutionary War, Connecticut volunteers.

The Parks family was involved in the lumber business in Ohio, but it did not suit Solomon. When he was twenty-six, he made his way to the California gold rush. Along with his cousin Nathan, he worked in the goldfields of El Dorado County, panning two dollars a day

How long he stayed in California is unclear. According to the *Lemhi Herald* of Salmon, by the 1860s, Parks was in South Africa working in the diamond fields. While there, he said he was shot by a highwayman who robbed him and left him for dead. Once Parks recovered from his wounds and returned to the United States, he continued to seek his fortune in mining. In 1875 he reportedly was in the Black Hills of South Dakota, where he remained for two years. At some time during his travels, Parks married. By the time he made it to Idaho, however, he was a widower.

In 1877, when he reached Salmon City, he immediately headed to the gold mines along the river, working his own claims from Indianola to Shoup. Although he worked alone, he was well respected by other miners along the river and made friends with many of them.

As the years of hard work wore him thin, Parks was forced to abandon mining as a livelihood. In 1894 he went to work for his friend Charlie Spayd, who owned the way station at Indianola. Parks worked for him as a handyman for the next eight years. Then in fall 1901, he became so ill that he was bedridden. Spayd looked after him until Parks' death on March 5, 1902. The next day, with a group of friends, Spayd buried him behind the way station. Parks was the first burial in what became the Indianola cemetery.

His principle claim was located opposite Indian Creek on the Salmon River. A small stream there still bears his name.

William Verges

Even in rich gold country, mining is back-breaking—often depends on luck. William "Wild Bill" Verges learned this early in his days on the Salmon River and spent most of his time trying to find something else to do to make a living.

Verges, also spelled Vergis, was born in February 1852, in Michigan to German immigrant parents. How long he stayed with his family is unknown, but he began moving westward in the 1870s. By 1880 he was living on the Dearborn River in Montana making a marginal living as a miller. The 1880 census reported that he had been out of work for seven months.

Without work and fewer prospects, Verges eventually made his way to Idaho. In 1900 he was working as a carpenter in Salmon and living with a partner, Henry Smith. This time, he had been unemployed for six months. He tried his hand at mining but appears to have enjoyed little success. In 1902 he sold one-half interest in the Woodchuck quartz claim to his friend Charles Spayd for one dollar.

How and why Verges acquired his nickname "Wild Bill" is unclear. He was fairly well known in Salmon and along the river west to Shoup, and his comings and goings were often reported in the *Lemhi Herald*. In October 1903, Verges acquired the mail route between Indianola and Shoup. Perhaps the work was too difficult or the pay insufficient, because he only kept the job six weeks. By January 1904, his new job was maintaining the phone line between Ulysses

William Verges is buried in the northeast corner of the cemetery at Indianola Ranger Station.

and North Fork. He kept this job for several years, yet was always seeking other ways to improve his fortune.

In spring 1904, Verges obtained a contract to dam the

Salmon River and install generators that would power all of the machinery along the river. He hired men and planned to use the telephone poles to run the electrical lines. Like many well-laid plans, however, this one fell through.

In 1908 Verges settled near Indianola. In August he ran a notice in the *Lemhi Herald*, seeking a woman who would can fruit for him for either a salary or shares. Either no woman accepted his offer, or if one did, she did not suit him, because on February 11, 1909, he was in Salmon, where he announced he was heading to Montana in search of a wife. He sold his last piece of property, the Little Horse Lode, and left town with $100.

Whether Verges ever reached Montana is unknown, but if he did, he should have stayed there. Instead, he returned to Indianola and within two weeks, he was dead.

Verges' death occurred on February 24, 1909. Stories of the circumstances disagree. One says that he jumped some claims on Indian Creek belonging to Charles Layton. Layton caught him and killed him.

Another story was told by Layton, who called the *Lemhi Herald* to report Verges' death. Layton said he and Verges were in the middle of a fight, with Verges using the butt of his six-shooter to beat Layton on his head. Layton's son, Roy, interrupted, grabbed his father's pistol, and killed Verges.

Roy and Charles Layton were charged with manslaughter, but once the crime was investigated by the sheriff, the charges against Roy Layton were dropped. Charles Layton, however, was charged with willful murder.

He went to trial in Salmon on April 22, 1909. Jury selection took three days. The court record has been lost, but the prosecutor argued that Layton killed Verges and then persuaded his son to tell the self-defense story. The Laytons took the witness stand in their own defense. On the afternoon of April 28, 1909, the jury received its instructions. It deliberated all night and at 5:00 a.m. returned a guilty verdict.

Layton was sentenced to twenty-five years hard labor at the Idaho State Penitentiary in Boise. His son Roy, only ten, was committed to the reform school at St. Anthony, Idaho.

An inquest was held at Indianola. The Lemhi County coroner confirmed that the cause of death was a gunshot wound, and noted Verges' personal property: thirty-five cents and a chest of carpenter's tools. The coroner turned the money over to the Lemhi County treasurer.

Verges was buried in the Indianola cemetery, and today a wooden headboard marks his grave.

Charles Spayd

Once called by a reporter the "grand pooh-bah and lord" of Indianola, Charlie Spayd, nevertheless, could not overcome his own demons.

C. H. Spayd, as he was often called, was born in Pennsylvania on November 23, 1853, the son of John and Kate Spayd. He lived there during his early years, residing in Reading, Pennsylvania, until 1880. Shortly thereafter, Spayd made his way to Idaho and the Salmon River.

He settled on an acreage that over the years changed names

from the Big Flat Ranch, to the Spayd Ranch, to the Spayd-Wend Ranch. Located five miles northeast of Shoup on the north side of the Salmon River, it was ideal for a garden and for raising cattle. Soon Spayd found himself supplying miners with fresh fruits, vegetables, and meat. Although profitable, the work was not all that agreeable. He took Thomas Wend as a partner, selling him one-half interest in the place in June 1888 for $2,000. Wend gradually assumed complete responsibility for the ranch.

In the fall of 1887, Spayd moved to the mouth of Indian Creek, and over the next seventeen years it was his primary residence. He established a business more suited to his disposition: a hotel and tavern serving miners on their way to Shoup or Ulysses. Over the years he added a livery stable and a blacksmith's shop. The place also served as a hunting lodge.

Spayd became active in politics, serving as county commissioner from District III of Lemhi County from 1887 to 1889. In 1888 he ran for Lemhi County assessor as a Republican but lost. He did not run for public office again, but he did remain active in the Republican party, sometimes serving as a delegate to the Lemhi County and Idaho Republican conventions.

Spayd and his establishment became a regional attraction. Generous to a fault, he usually attended to the needs of others rather than to his own. His mining claims never proved profitable; consequently, most of his energies went into the waystation at Indianola, where he served as mayor, postmaster, barber, and sometimes deputy sheriff. Over the years his problem drinking and his erratic behavior took a toll.

In early 1900, Spayd began making regular trips to Salmon. While he made the trips on the pretext of business, he also had another purpose in mind: Mary Finley. On January 9, 1904, he married her, and the couple returned to Indianola.

Newlywed bliss was short-lived. Mary, either unaware of Charlie's problems or persuaded she could change him, was unnerved by his behavior. By February she was back in Salmon and complained to a local reporter that her husband was going crazy. While they remained married for three years, it was a tumultuous relationship, and they were apart more than they were together.

In March of 1905, Mary moved to Salmon for the summer. She reported that Charlie was going to lease the waystation for six months. He, however, had different plans. On March 16, 1905, he sold the place and the mining claim that accompanied it to Charles Layton for $1,380. Then Spayd moved to Salmon.

For a year he traveled to mining areas in the county: Shoup, Camp Ramey, Pine Creek, North Fork. Although his marriage had obviously failed, in March 1906 he stopped in Salmon to check on Mary. Afterwards, he went to Butte, Montana, to live. Since he was no longer living in Idaho, the Lemhi County Republican Party replaced him as central committeeman for the Ulysses district.

In Montana, Spayd's behavior became even less predictable. In January 1907, while in Dillon, Montana, he attempted to take his own life by cutting his wrists and throat and then stabbing himself in the heart. Bleeding profusely, he staggered into the Mint Saloon, where he collapsed. A doctor was summoned, but the wounds proved superficial. For his own protection, Spayd was thrown in jail. Close

C. H. Spayd, the founder of Indianola, is buried in the cemetery located just north of the Indianola Ranger Station.

friends observed that Spayd appeared insane and prone to violence. He attributed it to alcohol and wrote a long letter to his wife swearing that he would never drink again. He traveled to Oklahoma, where he moved in with a brother and did his best to overcome his habit.

Mary Spayd, tired of her husband's conduct, filed for divorce. Court proceedings began in April 1907. Three separate summons were sent to Spayd regarding the divorce, but he never responded. On October 1, 1907, the divorce was granted.

True to his word, Spayd quit drinking. When he returned to Salmon in March 1908, the *Lemhi Herald* reported that he was looking "first rate" and was happy to be back in the community. He traveled downriver, staked new claims, and revived old friendships. A letter in the *Lemhi Herald* revealed a renewed interest in political issues, as he voiced his opinion on the building site for the new county courthouse.

Yet despite his efforts at reform, Spayd could not break the grip of insanity. Reports reached Salmon that he was increasingly mad. Among his strange behaviors, he stripped naked and then threw his clothes into the river. Although friends looked after him, they were unable to protect him from himself.

Two conflicting versions of Spayd's last day exist. One says that he went to the Wend Ranch to inquire about work. Not finding anyone at the home, he broke into the place, stole a rifle, walked to the riverbank, and shot himself. Wend, who had been working in a distant field, saw a man walking to the edge of the river but did not recognize him as Spayd. When the man fell, Wend ran to help but was too late.

Another says that Spayd had been living with Wend. Wend left for Ulysses with a load of vegetables for the miners, and while he was gone, Spayd went out into a field near the house and shot himself. Wend found him when he returned.

Spayd's death was investigated by Charles Hammer, Lemhi County coroner. He concluded that Spayd died on May 9, 1909, from the effects of a gunshot wound. His report says that the wound was self-inflicted by Spayd while he was temporarily deranged.

Spayd's body was returned to Indianola and buried behind his waystation. An impressive stone marks his grave, although the person responsible for placing it there is now forgotten.

James McConn

While several of the gravesites along the Salmon River belong to veterans, only James McConn's grave is marked with a military stone.

McConn was born on December 19, 1847, in West Alexander, Pennsylvania. During his childhood, his family moved south to West Virginia, and he grew up and helped on the family farm there.

The family was still in West Virginia at the outbreak of the Civil War. On August 19, 1862, McConn, only fourteen, enlisted in the Union Army at Wheeling, West Virginia, for a three-year tour of duty. Although his enlistment papers said he was eighteen, his small stature revealed otherwise. Five feet, four inches, with black hair, brown eyes, and a dark complexion, he was still a boy. He was assigned to Company C, 12th West Virginia Volunteer Infantry and given the rank of private.

James McConn's military headstone unlocked the secrets to his past.

As a member of the 12th Infantry, his early service involved guarding and escorting Union supply trains between battlefields. He narrowly missed the Battle of Gettysburg, but was at Bloody Run, Pennsylvania, on June 30, 1863. He avoided the carnage of battle during his first year of service, but he could not escape other miseries. He was stricken with illness, and in 1864 spent six months in military hospitals at Winchester and Martinsburg, West Virginia.

When he recovered in January 1865, he rejoined his unit. He spent the next four months in Virginia with his company, following the lead of General Ulysses Grant in pursuit of Robert E. Lee. When Lee surrendered in Richmond on April 9, 1865, McConn was present. On June 16, 1865, McConn was mustered out of service, a few months before his eighteenth birthday. He left the service four inches taller than when he enlisted and was $75 richer.

He traveled westward, stopping first in Illinois for three years, then moving to Iowa, for ten years of farming. The lure of the west still beckoned, and in 1878 he came as far as Wyoming. Over the next nineteen years, he spent time in Wyoming , South Dakota, and Idaho, before firmly settling in Idaho around 1898.

McConn is listed in the 1890 federal census of veterans. At that time he was living in Bear Gulch, South Dakota, and declared he was in good health. In 1895, however, while living in Freemont County, Wyoming, he filed for a military disability pension as allowed under the Pension Act of June 27, 1890. In his petition he declared that he was unable to earn a living by manual labor because of a lung disease and general disability. He filed his claim in November 1895, with two letters of support from acquaintances. In June his claim was rejected.

Undeterred, in August 1896, McConn filed again from Big Horn County, Wyoming. This time a doctor backed up his claim. In his report, Dr. R. W. Hale stated that McConn had diseases of the heart and right lung causing him shortness of breath and a bad cough. He added that even the slightest exertion caused McConn to spit blood and described McConn as shrunken, with flabby, loose muscles and dull, sunken eyes. The doctor concluded his report stating "this veteran cannot smell at all and is almost deaf." A year later, McConn's application was approved, entitling him to a pension of $10 per month.

McConn left Wyoming and headed north to Idaho. Arriving in Salmon, he worked his way to the mining districts around Shoup and Ulysses. The mountain climate must have been McConn's cure because soon he was buying and working mining claims around Ulysses. Gradually he moved northwest from Ulysses and made a copper strike: the Copper Queen mine. He held this claim and an interest in the Lucky Cuss Mine until his death.

By 1908 McConn was fairly well recognized among the miners along the Salmon River. He traveled frequently from Salmon City to his mining claims northwest on Indian Creek. In November 1908, McConn supervised the election returns from Ulysses all the way to Salmon City. After depositing the ballots in Salmon, he floated downstream with Salmon River boatman Harry Guleke, back to his claims.

McConn's name appears in the 1910 federal census for Lemhi County. He said he was working as a gold miner and owned his own home. In July that year, he refiled for his military pension under the Pension Act of February 6, 1907. The request granted, his pension increased to $12 a month.

McConn's raise was short-lived, however. On March 23, 1911, the death registry of Lemhi County listed his passing, caused by chronic Bright's Disease (kidneys). He was buried at the Indianola cemetery. His death was not reported in the *Lemhi Herald* until May 25, 1911. On August 31, 1911, his property was sold at public auction.

A trail still leads to the Copper Queen Mine, and a tributary bearing McConn's name runs into Indian Creek, which flows past his grave on its way to the Salmon River.

Henry Merritt

Henry Clay Merritt was on his way to becoming one of the leading citizens of Lemhi County. A young man with an educated wife and two beautiful children, Merritt's life ended tragically on the Salmon River.

Merritt was born in Kentucky on June 4, 1843. The Merritts were an extensive clan in Kentucky, but Henry chose to strike out on his own at an early age.

He left the hollows of Kentucky for the goldfields of Nevada, arriving in Lander County in the late 1860s. He met Ada Chase there; she had emigrated to Nevada from Michigan in 1864 with her parents, who bought a ranch and grazed stock throughout the state and into Idaho Territory. On March 3, 1870, Henry and Ada married in Austin, Nevada. He was 26; she was 18.

Their first child, Emma, was born a year later. Their son, Allen, followed seven years later.

Merritt traded mining for work in the cattle business. His job often forced him to leave his wife and children at home. In the 1880 federal census, Henry was in Oneida County in southeast Idaho, where he reported that he was married but living by himself.

In 1881 Henry's parents migrated to Shoup, Idaho, because of the gold boom there. Henry took an interest too, because he made several trips to Lemhi County and invested heavily in mines in the Leesburg District. In May of 1882, Henry, together with five other men, paid $8,000 for a $1/5$ interest in the Golden Rule, Golden Terra, Musgrove, Arnett, Comet, and Albion mines. In August 1883, Henry, accompanied by his wife and children, moved to Salmon to engage in mining once again.

Henry Merritt is buried at Spring Creek Bar, 17.7 miles west of North Fork, Idaho. The grave is surrounded by a chain link fence on the south side of the road, just past the entrance to the Spring Creek campground.

He focused his attentions on the Mineral Hill Mining District near Shoup. Working several claims in the area, he was admired for his honesty and industriousness. He was named superintendent of the Kentuck Mine at Shoup.

Merritt soon learned that hauling supplies downriver on a sweep boat was more efficient than packing them overland on mules down the rough trail to Shoup. In November 1884, floating from Salmon to Shoup with a load of mining supplies, his sweep blade hit a rock near Indian Creek, and he was tossed overboard and drowned. His body surfaced several days later at Spring Creek, ten miles downstream. His family buried him there, marking the spot with the most elaborate headstone on the river.

Ada was forced to fend for herself. At age thirty-two, she bought the *Idaho Recorder*, the Salmon weekly newspaper, and became the first female editor in Idaho Territory. Their son, Allen, became an engineer, architect, and a leading surveyor in Lemhi County.

Joseph Laughlin

Joseph Laughlin was well-liked, a prosperous miner who owned several valuable claims along the Salmon River, including the California Mine, located across the river from Shoup, Idaho. Originally from the Chicago area, Laughlin arrived in Shoup in the early 1890s and began to develop mining claims there. He served as the postmaster of Shoup for several years, and a newspaper reported that he was "honorable, a good citizen, and a true friend."

On June 1, 1900, he met Charles Gale at Spring Creek Bar on the Salmon River. Laughlin had agreed to take Gale down river to Shoup in a small wooden boat. Gale had planned to spend some time at the hot springs near the Panther Creek trail. On the afternoon of June 1, 1900, after putting Gale ashore, Laughlin continued down the river.

Laughlin was reported missing on June 2. Friends searched the river banks for days and found only his overturned boat at the mouth of Dutch Oven Creek, six miles below Shoup. They concluded that Laughlin had capsized in Black Snake Rapids as he attempted to reach the north bank of the river.

A little over a month later, on July 4, Johnny McKay, a long-time Salmon River boatman-prospector, discovered Laughlin's body near the mouth of Long Tom Creek. McKay was on his way from the Middle Fork of the Salmon to Shoup, but he stopped long enough to bury Laughlin in a temporary grave. He walked on to Shoup and then to Spring Creek, where he notified Mark Quinlivan, a friend of Laughlin. Quinlivan had a ranch on Spring Creek.

He notified Laughlin's relatives in Illinois, and they decided Laughlin should be buried at Spring Creek. On October 4, W. W. St. Clair, James Stewart, and J. M. South left Salmon to retrieve the body. It took them five days. On October 9, 1900, funeral services were held for Laughlin, and he was reinterred on the bar. But his grave remains a mystery, because no stone or marker can now be found.

Upon Laughlin's death, Quinlivan was named the administrator of the estate. In July 1901, he sold all of

Laughlin's property to Hiram Haynes. It included five mining claims and a millsite, all located in the Mineral Hill Mining District. The sale netted $2,500. How Quinlivan distributed the proceeds was never reported.

John Burr

John Burr rests only twenty feet from the Salmon River Road at the north end of the Cove Creek Bridge, twenty-eight miles west of North Fork, Idaho.

Johnny Burr is buried at the north end of the Cove Creek Bridge, 28.5 miles west of North Fork.

Where Burr was born or where he lived before coming to the Salmon River is unknown now. He is not listed in any Idaho or Montana census. While several men named Burr traveled from Montana to the mining areas of Shoup, none of them had "John" or "Johnny" as a first name.

The only clue lies in a delinquent tax list for Lemhi County in 1896, noting that the property of J. W. Burr of Gibbonsville was to be sold at public auction to satisfy the taxes. On July 6, 1896, the property-a house valued at - purchased by the county for $14.65.

Within a year, Burr drowned in the Salmon River. He was traveling to Shoup on a supply scow with a friend, William Taylor. The day was warm, and Burr, an able swimmer, spent much of the trip cooling off in the river. When the boat landed at Shoup, Burr jumped into the river to secure the bow line. He never surfaced. His body was recovered near the mouth of Cove Creek, ten miles below Shoup.

A massive, black stone marks his grave, which is maintained by the U.S. Forest Service.

C. H. Daniels

The grave of Charles Henry Daniels lies on a wind-swept slope overlooking the Salmon River.

Daniels was born in Winneshiek, Iowa, in September 1873. He had one older brother, Leon, who was also born in Iowa. Daniels' parents were from New York.

In the early 1890s, Charles and Leon traveled west to

The grave of C. H. Daniels is clearly visible across the river from the Salmon River Road, three-quarters of a mile west of the Cove Creek Bridge.

California, where they settled in Napa. There Charles met Abbie M. Jacks, and on March 2, 1895, they married. He was twenty-one; Abbie was eighteen.

They stayed in Napa for the next few years. In 1899 a daughter, Ethel, was born. In the 1900 census, Daniels states they lived on Main Street in Napa, where he worked as a druggist. Leon was living with them.

Charles' life between 1900 and 1919 is a mystery, but in 1920, he was working as a millwright in a camp operated by the Siletz Logging Company in Polk County, Oregon. His wife and daughter were not with him.

He left Polk County and drifted to Grants Pass, Oregon. He remarried. His second wife, Mary, was fourteen years younger than he. They had one son, James. To support his family, Daniels worked as a carpenter.

In 1933 the family moved to Idaho, arriving in Salmon a year later. They settled at Shoup where Daniels continued to work as a carpenter. He also tried mining, becoming partners with Fred Snook, well known in Lemhi County for his land and mining deals. Daniels staked one claim on his own, the Million Dollar Color Claim No. 1. Located near the mouth of Panther Creek, it extended 6,000 feet east along the Salmon River. Daniels held this property at the time of his death.

On November 23, 1943, he died at home. The coroner listed the cause of death as "natural causes due to age."

Funeral services were held in Shoup, after which Daniels was taken downriver to the south end of the Cove Creek bridge. From there he was carried three quarters of a mile west of the bridge above a large rock outcropping. His grave was marked with a black granite stone still visible today.

Edward Gwyther

Downriver, fourteen miles west of Shoup, Lake Creek flows into the Main Salmon. Ed Gwyther made his home at the mouth of the creek.

Little is known about his past. He was born in Utah,

probably around 1888, and had at least two brothers. Both of his parents were from England, and his father was a farmer.

Gwyther served in Michigan's 4th Infantry in World War I. According to the Salmon *Recorder Herald*, Gwyther was wounded in action, and military records report that he received a veteran's pension.

He arrived in Idaho in the 1920s and apparently wandered from site to site along the river until 1930, when he purchased property at the mouth of Lake Creek on the south side of the river. There he did some placer mining and farmed the bar. He kept mostly to himself, but Gwyther was well liked by his neighbors.

In July 1934, while Captain Harry Guleke was taking a party down the Salmon River from Salmon to Lewiston, he stopped at Gwyther's cabin and found Gwyther dead in his bed, his two dogs standing guard. Guleke sent a messenger to summon the coroner who made a trip downriver to the site.

Coroner William Doebler arrived on August 4 and determined that Gwyther had died on July 29, probably of a heart attack. Then Doebler, along with three men from Guleke's party, buried Gwyther near the riverbank. If a marker was placed on the grave, it has since washed away.

The coroner notified Jack Gwyther in Colorado of his brother's death. Jack moved to the river and took over the farm. He died in 1938 and is buried in the Salmon cemetery.

Coy Lansbury

Lantz Bar is situated forty-seven miles west of North Fork, Idaho, on an extremely isolated part of the Salmon River. This isolation contributed to Coy Lansbury's death.

Lansbury, whose name has also been recorded as Lansbery, was born February 3, 1910, the son of Claud Lansbury of West Virginia. He arrived in Idaho in the fall of 1927 and traveled to Lantz Bar to stay with his cousin Frank Lantz, who had settled on the bar a year earlier.

Coy Lansbury's grave can be found approximately 100 yards west of the guard station at Lantz Bar.

In the spring of 1928, Lansbury became ill with what appeared to be Rocky Mountain Spotted Fever. He was too sick to journey to Salmon on his own to see a doctor, so Lantz made the trip to Salmon to obtain medicine. While he was gone, Lansbury died.

Lansbury's body was discovered by John Cunningham, who buried him on the west edge of the bar and marked the spot with two flat tones. Today, a pyramid-shaped stone with a bronze marker pays tribute to the young man.

A Forest Service report written in 1970 mentions a grave on the bar belonging to a child or grandchild of Mitt Haynie, who lived at Lantz Bar prior to 1925. Whether this refers to the Lansbury grave or whether there is actually another grave on the bar is not clear.

Hugo Vater

The Salmon River can be a rough boat ride even for experienced river rats. The early miners and settlers along the river were aware of the risks and traveled by foot rather than risk the unpredictable rapids. Those who knew the river respected its power.

Some, however, dared the river for a living. Harry Guleke of Salmon was one. Guleke made a name for himself navigating the river in his wooden sweep boats, hauling freight and supplies to residents down the river for nearly forty years. His success lured others to attempt the same feat, including Hugo Vater.

Vater was born in Germany on August 29, 1881. He made his way to the United States around the turn of the century, probably disembarking in San Francisco. From there he traveled to Twin Falls County, Idaho. Eventually, he homesteaded a site near Rogerson, a small community twenty-nine miles southwest of Twin Falls. It was the gateway to a rich mining district immediately across the Idaho-Nevada state line.

Vater never became a United States citizen, although he did register for the draft at the outbreak of World War I. In his registration papers, he declared himself an alien, a citizen of Germany, self-employed as a carpenter. He was blue-eyed and brown-haired with a slender build.

While in Rogerson, Vater teamed with Robert G. Hoffman. Together they worked their adjacent homesteads. In 1928 the two were living together in Oil Town, an arrangement that ended only with Vater's death.

In the spring of 1933, Vater and Hoffman decided to leave their homesteads and try placer mining on the Salmon River. Arriving in Salmon in late June, they built a sweep boat measuring seven by twenty-one feet, and three feet high. Framed with 4 x 6's and double-hulled, the boat was loaded with enough food to last a year and tools to operate a placer claim. In early July, the two men set out on their journey down the River of No Return.

Slowly, they made their way down the river. On August 15, they approached Black Canyon Falls, now known as Salmon Falls. As the boat entered the rapid, it struck a rock, lurched violently sideways, and Hoffman, on the front sweep, held on for his life. When he regained his footing, he looked back, and Vater was gone.

With the boat through the rapid, Hoffman now searched the river for his friend and spotted him seventy-five feet downstream. According to Hoffman, he dived into the water to attempt a rescue, but the current sucked Vater down before he could be reached. He never reappeared.

Hoffman pulled his boat out at Sabe Creek, one mile below the falls, and for the next four days wandered along the river seeking help. At Bear Creek, five miles downriver, he found Monroe Hancock. He helped Hoffman get his boat down to the South Fork where he traded it to some miners for a pack ride to Warren. From there he made his way home.

Vater's body surfaced at Hot Springs Bar, just below what is now known as Barth Hot Springs. Hoffman reported that it was found on August 27 by Maisie Hancock. How he learned the date is not clear. Vater's death certificate lists the date as August 15, 1933, with burial at the hot springs on August 16. His death was reported to the authorities by Sarah Ayres. He was buried by the Hancocks, who placed a small wooden cross on the grave. Over time, both the cross and the location have been lost.

Anthony March

In summer 1934, the Salmon River flowed uncommonly low. A light snowpack the previous winter and scant rainfall in the spring turned the Salmon into a tangle of exposed rocks that gave new challenges to even the most experienced river runners. Anthony March was not an experienced river runner; he challenged the river and lost.

Of all the men buried along the river, he is the least known. March appears in only two public records: in a newspaper story that relates the circumstances of his death, and in his death certificate, on file with the Idaho Department of Vital Statistics. These, however, fail to reveal who he really was. He was about thirty-five years old, single, and lived in North Fork, Idaho, at the time of his death. His death certificate states his name as Anthony Marsh.

March and his partner, Bill E. Miller, were taking a load of lumber on a large sweepboat downstream from North Fork to an unknown location. They reached Salmon Falls on July 25. As they attempted to raft through the left channel, they lost control and smashed into the rocks. Both men were thrown into the water. The boat broke into pieces, its frame washed up on a rock in the middle of the river a half mile below the falls.

Miller and March survived the wreck and tried to salvage some of their lumber from the waters below the falls. March lost his footing and was pulled into a deep hole, where he drowned.

His body surfaced twelve days later just below present-day Barth Hot Springs. On August 7, Captain Harry Guleke and several others who were on an expedition down the river, found March's body and buried it on the bench above the springs. No marker was placed at the grave, and today only the general location is known.

Thomas Newson

Of all the spirits of the Salmon River, Thomas Newson had a head start on the way to his heaven.

Information about him is vague. Where and when he was born, his parentage, and his entire life are all mysterious. No records exist in Idaho, Oregon, or Washington. He *is* buried on the Salmon River.

Newson came to Idaho as a tenant farmer, following his sister-in-law, Emma Zaunmiller, and her husband, Joe Zaunmiller, to the secluded ranches along the Salmon River near Dixie, Idaho. The Zaunmillers worked at various ranches along the river, including the Harbison-Cook and the Allison, before settling at Campbell's Ferry.

Newson resided at the Crofoot Ranch, about one and one-half miles north of the river, up Rattlesnake Creek. The ranch was homesteaded by Bruce Crofoot, who left it in 1926. Shortly thereafter, Newson arrived with his wife, Louisa, their young daughter, and their dog, "Chubby." Frank and Bessie Santos, former owners of the Crofoot Ranch, have a picture of Newson and his dog taken there in 1927.

Shortly after this—the date is uncertain—Newson died. One account asserts the death occurred after he had a tooth extracted in Grangeville. When he returned to the ranch, he got an infection and died.

Forest Service records indicate Newson is buried on the north end of the Crofoot airstrip. Two venerable apple trees stand on the west side of the runway, and Newson's grave lies under the northern-most tree. Bessie Santos said that at one time the Forest Service planned to mark the grave with a headboard but never did.

A fairly steep trail up from the mouth of Rattlesnake Creek at the Salmon brings the visitor to the south end of the Crofoot landing strip. At the ranch nothing now remains except corner markers for the old cabin. The boundless view and the majestic Ponderosas standing like spires make the Crofoot Ranch and Newson's resting place heaven on earth.

Thaddeus Rucker

Near Split Rock Rapid on the Main Salmon lies the grave of Thaddeus "Ed" Rucker, whose story is known only because his killer had a guilty conscience.

Rucker was born in Lawrence County, Ohio. In the 1890s he left his home in Scot Town, Ohio, and headed west, supposedly to try his hand at mining.

Before he arrived in Idaho County, he worked in Spokane, Washington, as a barber. He earned a reputation there as moody, if not a little peculiar. When barbering did not work out, he headed to Salmon City, where he hired on with a railroad survey party. He served as a boatman for the survey crew and, consequently, knew the river well.

During that year with the survey, he had the opportunity to examine sites along the river and found one to his liking: Butts Bar, now known as Cunningham Bar, located across the river from Corn Creek, launch site for most Main Salmon trips. Rucker settled there, probably in 1909, and filed a homestead application on the place.

In June of 1910, Forest Ranger Walter Mann traveled to the Salmon River to survey Rucker's homestead. He was fascinated by stories he had heard about the "wild man" who grew his hair long, had a full beard, never wore a hat, and ran away when people approached. Mann, accompanied by Warren Cook and Ted McCall, met Rucker on Butts Bar, and although Mann described Rucker as an eccentric old fellow, sour and grouchy, he also wrote that he looked a lot like Jesus Christ. Mann noted in his report that except for some dried meat Rucker had hanging by his fireplace, he was out of food.

After Mann completed the homestead survey, Rucker took the three men downriver in a sweepboat to Disappointment Creek, where they had left their horses in the care of Jesse Root, owner of the Root Ranch on Whimstick Creek in Chamberlain Basin. There they gave Rucker a haircut, a shave, and enough provisions to get him back to Salmon City, where he insisted he was going. Mann returned to McCall and did the paper work on the homestead, but Rucker did not live long enough to obtain the patent.

In Salmon City, he met Samuel Pruitt, and the two began a partnership, trapping and mining in the Salmon River Mountains.

In May of 1911, Rucker and Pruitt were on the Salmon, probably on Butts Bar, where their prospecting met with some success. As winter approached, the two turned their attentions to trapping. They brought in supplies, established a trap line, then settled into Rucker's cabin for the winter.

Rucker's surly personality made him as unpredictable as a grizzly. In the year they had been together, Pruitt had always been able to resolve disputes, but on the morning of November 5, 1911, Rucker woke up in a rage. Threatening to kill Pruitt, he went to the woodpile and grabbed an ax. Pruitt snatched his Winchester and started running, only to be chased. He turned and fired. The bullet passed through Rucker's arm and into his chest, killing him instantly.

Pruitt, desperate, decided to dispose of the body by weighting it with rocks and heaving it into the river. Shortly afterwards, Pruitt headed downriver to Edward Eakin's place, now known as Lantz Bar, and confessed his story. Eakin advised him to go to Grangeville and turn himself in to the sheriff. Meanwhile, several miners went up river to Pruitt's camp to search the river for the body, but they failed to find it.

Arriving in Grangeville, Pruitt told his story and was promptly jailed. For the next three weeks, the sheriff investigated, gathering character information on both men. He also searched the river without success. Character witnesses from all parts of the country, including Rucker's own father in Ohio, confirmed Pruitt's assertion of self-defense. Because no body was recovered and no witnesses came forward, Pruitt was released on January 1, 1912. The case was dismissed.

In May 1912, a trio of bear hunters pulling a boat up the Salmon River discovered Rucker's body about a mile below Sam Myers' ranch, now the Allison Ranch. They identified it by the bullet hole through his arm and chest and a rope tied around his stomach. Truman Thomas and C. H. Prescott, both living on Richardson Bar at the time, buried the body where it was found, as requested by the county sheriff.

Immediately after he was released from jail, Pruitt left Idaho County and never returned. Rucker's grave was never marked and its exact location has been lost.

Truman Thomas

The Salmon River offered Truman Thomas a second chance at a good life. He took it and lived his last fifteen years at Yellow Pine Bar on the banks of the Salmon River.

Thomas was born in New York in 1846, the same state in which his parents were born. How long he stayed in the East is unknown, but eventually a job with the railroad took him to all parts of the country.

While in the Midwest, he married and had three children, Mildred and Shirley, and a son, Truman, Jr. The son, born in Nebraska in 1885 and known as "Kid," was his last child.

Alcoholism destroyed Thomas' marriage and his career. In the 1890s, he found his way to Spokane, Washington. Attempting to start over, he left his son in the care of friends and headed east to the mining areas of Idaho.

Shortly after the turn of the century, Thomas took the trail from Dixie south to the Salmon River. Crossing the river at Campbell's Ferry, he followed the Three Blaze Trail until it climbed Ramey Ridge. He built a cabin near the ridge and over the next few years filed several mining claims in the vicinity. In May of 1904, he partnered with Virgil Richardson, for whom Richardson Bar on the Salmon River is named, and filed on the May Placer on Mulligan Creek. Three months later, he went into a partnership with C. L. Danforth to file War Eagle 1 and 2 on the West Fork of Ramey Creek.

In 1909 Truman's son joined him, and they moved closer to the Salmon River. They must have found an especially rich pocket near Lick Creek, since they filed two claims there. In September they filed the Independence Placer, a forty-acre claim located one mile south of Campbell's Ferry. Three months later they established a twenty-acre claim at the mouth of Lick Creek.

Perhaps father and son had a disagreement or the Lick claims were not as lucrative as they anticipated, because two years later, Kid Thomas left the river, and Truman was staking claims elsewhere. He traveled north upstream from Campbell's Ferry, where he discovered a high bench on the north side of the Salmon, which he named Yellow Pine Bar. It proved to be the site where he would spend the rest of his life.

In July of 1912, Thomas, along with C. H. Prescott and others, staked a 120-acre claim at the mouth of Richardson Creek, extending 4,000 feet east along the south bank of the Salmon. Thomas built a small cabin here and lived in it for the next several years. He began corresponding with a cousin, Celeste Strobreck of New York. Thomas learned that she suffered from ill health, and he invited her to live with him in Idaho. She accepted his offer and arrived sometime after 1912. They found they were compatible and in October 1914, they married in Dixie, Idaho. Clarence Churchill and C. H. Prescott served as witnesses.

In August 1914—a month before his marriage to Celeste—
Thomas staked the Gold Bar placer claim of forty acres
directly across the river from Richardson Creek. The claim
ran east-west, 2,000 feet along the north bank of the Salmon
on what Truman called "Yellow Pine Bar."

In summer 1915, Truman and Celeste moved into a cabin
he had built on the bar. That July he filed a homestead
application for the place. Meeting legal requirements, he
cleared the land, planted an orchard, and built a new cabin.
He dug irrigation ditches from a nearby spring, which also
supplied water to the house. When the homestead title was
finally issued in March of 1922, Truman and Celeste had
carved out a comfortable life for themselves on the bar.

Celeste and Truman were both in their seventies by then,
but they had no desire to leave the bar. Many of their
neighbors were friends, especially the Zaunmillers at
Campbell's Ferry, who often checked on the couple. Truman,
anticipating his death on the river, dug his own grave and
built his own pine coffin. Celeste kept it under their bed and
used it as a sewing chest until it was needed.

In January of 1930 for ten dollars, the couple bought
another homestead, the Logan Ranch, from William Logan.
It was 106 acres and alongside the trail to Elk City.

Only four months later, on May 3, 1930, Truman Thomas
died. Dr. A. W. Boyd of Red River, Idaho, was present and
listed kidney failure as the cause of death.

On the day he died, Truman Thomas dictated his will to
Emma Zaunmiller. The will, hand written on 3 x 5" tablet
paper, was witnessed by Dr. Boyd and John McCoy. Truman

left one dollar to each of his children. He left everything else to Celeste.

Truman was buried the next day, southwest of the house on the bank above the river. No marker was placed at the grave, and the exact location is now uncertain.

Celeste was the administrator of Truman's estate. Yellow Pine Bar and the Logan Ranch were valued at $700. He also had personal property valued at $200, including two cows, a horse, and $18 in the bank.

Without Truman, Celeste had no intention of staying on the river. Even before Truman's estate was settled, she sold the site to Charlie Ayres, who paid her $350 for it on February 6, 1931. Shortly after, Celeste left Idaho to live with her daughter in Minnesota. Four years later, she sold the Logan Ranch to M. A. Cook for one dollar.

Although Yellow Pine Bar has changed hands many times since it was sold by Celeste Thomas, it remains one of the few private in-holdings along the "wild and scenic" reach of the Salmon River.

Clarence Eugene Churchill

An accident left C. E. Churchill with only one hand and this eventually caused his death.

Gene Churchill, as he was commonly known, was born in September 1857, in Rutland, Vermont. He was the son of W. B. and Mary Churchill. They operated a well-established lumber business in Rutland. Gene left Vermont and the family business, however, for greener prospects in Wisconsin and Minnesota.

In March 1884, Gene married Ella Nutting, a Wisconsin native. The marriage survived separation and tragedy. Shortly after the wedding, the couple moved to northern Minnesota, where he worked in the Mesabi Iron Range mines. How long he worked there is uncertain, but by 1897 he had moved to Idaho, leaving his wife behind.

Once in Idaho, Churchill made his way to the Salmon River. He staked several mining claims along the river, one of them near Slate Creek. Here an accident cost him his left hand. According to an article in the December 23, 1898, issue of the *Idaho County Free Press*, he was working a claim with his partner W. H. Robertson, when a slope caved in. Churchill's left hand was pinned beneath a large boulder, nearly severing it between the wrist and knuckles. Robertson, also trapped beneath the rubble, was unable to help. Desperate, Churchill used a knife to extricate himself. He applied a tourniquet, then freed Robertson; Robertson then took Gene to John Day Creek, where Dr. Wilson Foskett amputated the remainder of Churchill's wrist. He was then fitted with a prosthetic leather harness and hook.

Following the accident, Churchill rode to the Elk City-Dixie area, where he was befriended by several men from the Salmon River, including William Campbell, owner of Campbell's Ferry. Churchill assisted Campbell in building the first cabin at the Ferry. He also staked additional mining claims.

The 1900 census verifies Churchill was in Dixie and that

he and Ella were still separated. Churchill stated that he was a gold miner and also a widow. In Minnesota, however, Ella recorded that she was married and caring for an adopted daughter, Stella Zahn Churchill. This discrepancy has never been explained, but by 1901, Ella had joined her husband on the Salmon.

On January 1, 1901, Gene filed for two mining claims at the mouth of Little Mallard Creek: Reno 1 and 2. The placer claims were twenty acres each and eventually became known as the Churchill Ranch. Over the next ten years, Gene and Ella worked hard on the place. They cleared the bar and diverted water from Little Mallard Creek for irrigation. In addition to growing a large garden, they planted alfalfa and fruit trees and raised cattle and dairy cows.

The Churchills soon had a thriving business providing the miners in Dixie, Elk City, and Thunder Mountain with fresh fruit, vegetables, and meat. Gene Churchill was among the few packers to take supplies into Thunder Mountain, a difficult job. With his ranch on the north side of the river, and the trail on the south, he made three trips across the river to get the pack horses and supplies to the other side. Once this was accomplished, he made the fifty-mile trip in five days.

Churchill also served as a guide to newcomers, leading miners and hunters along trails to and from Thunder Mountain. The ranch was a welcome sight to travelers, as he and Ella often accommodated visitors without charge.

The Churchills lived their lives on the bar until tragedy came in the fall of 1915.

In mid-September, Gene purchased a wooden boat from its owner on Rattlesnake Creek, nine miles upriver from the ranch. Gene, Truman Thomas, and C. H. Prescott went there to bring the boat down. The float back was uneventful until they approached Richardson Bar, where they struck a rock in the middle of the river. The boat filled with water, and the three of them were stranded on the rock. Their yells eventually attracted Celeste Thomas, who was near the Thomas cabin on Yellow Pine Bar. She went upriver to get help from Sam Myers, who lived at the present-day Allison Ranch. By the time she and Myers arrived to attempt a rescue, it was dark. The three men remained stranded overnight.

At daylight, Myers, Vic Bargamin, and Ed Harbison waded to the rescue. Sources disagree about what happened. One account states that Thomas and Prescott were rescued first, with ropes thrown to the rock; they were then pulled to shore. Finally it was Churchill's turn. He tied the rope to his hook. As he was pulled toward shore, the leather straps attaching the hook to his forearm broke. Churchill, unable to swim in such turbulence with one arm, went under and was drowned. In another account, although the manner of the accident is the same, it states rescuers first attempted to save Churchill. After he was lost, the other two men were rescued from the far side of the river.

Twenty-five days later, Churchill's body surfaced below the rapids. His friends buried him on Richardson Bar and then looked after Ella. She eventually remarried and filed for a homestead title on her place, which was issued in 1922.

Churchill's grave was marked by the Forest Service with

a wooden headboard, but with time it disappeared. A creek that parallels Little Mallard Creek to the west now bears his name, as does a mountain located five miles northwest of present-day Whitewater Ranch.

John Bergman

John Bergman was a gambler, and his gravesite on the Salmon River is simply the result of ill luck or good fortune.

Born in Minnesota in 1871, Bergman was the son of Swedish immigrants. He made his way west by the 1890s, spending time in Nevada, Oregon, Washington, and Idaho. He never stayed in one place too long.

During one of his sojourns to Troy, Idaho, he met the woman who agreed to become his wife. On April 25, 1899, Bergman married Anna Ferdlund. He was twenty-eight; she was nineteen. Together they had five children: sons Arthur and Burton, daughters Viva, Alga, and Reho.

Their home changed often; it seemed Bergman simply could not settle. They lived in Shotts, Montana; Denio and Enterprise, Oregon; and Fallon, Nevada. In Idaho, they spent time in Kamiah, Riggins, Jerome, Moscow, and Gooding. The places they lived were adequate at best; in Fallon, for example, the family lived in a one-room sod hut with a dirt floor. Bergman won the place in a poker game.

Bergman's addiction to gambling compelled him to leave his wife and children alone for long periods. Attempting to temper his absences and gambling losses, he sometimes provided Anna with a large house and a garden plot. For income, she could convert the place into a boarding house, and from the garden feed the children. According to grandson John Wolfe, nobody cared much for John Bergman.

When Bergman was not gambling, he was a farmer. In August of 1920, the family settled in Riggins, where he paid $700 for acreage with an orchard on the west side of the Little Salmon River. He planted a large garden and for the next few years provided for his family by selling produce in Riggins, Meadows Valley, and McCall. At times he hauled freight. Eventually, his gambling resumed. He lost the house, and the family was forced to move yet again.

Through the 1920s and 1930s, Bergman continued his nomadic life. His children grew up and left to establish their own lives. He fell on hard times. Anna, tired of putting up with his peripatetic ways, left to live with one of her children.

By 1945, suffering from diabetes and no longer able to take care of himself, Bergman decided to make his way to the Salmon River, where his daughter Reho lived. She was the only child willing to take him in.

In early June of that year, Bergman arrived in Elk City. Too sick to make it to the river on his own, he got a ride to the Dale Ranch (now the Whitewater Ranch) with the district forest ranger, who was heading down to the river to visit George Wolfe, Bergman's son-in-law. Wolfe had rounded up the Forest Service horses that wintered on the river. He and the ranger made their exchange; then Wolfe took Bergman to the Allison Ranch where he, Reho, and their two children, Norman and Carol, were living. Once they arrived, Reho made her father as comfortable as circumstances permitted.

Two weeks later, George Wolfe and Norman returned to the Dale Ranch to collect Bergman's luggage, which had been brought to the river by a friend. On the return trip home, young Norman slipped and fell into Big Mallard Creek. He was swept down into the swollen Salmon River and drowned.

Reho was grief stricken. Each day she walked the trail along the river, searching for Norman or his body. At the same time, her father's condition worsened. Realizing he was in need of immediate medical attention, she put him on a horse and headed downriver to the Dale Ranch. She planned

The grave of John Bergman is located on Richardson Bar, on the south side of the river, across from the Yellow Pine Bar airstrip. On Richardson Bar, the faint outline of an old cabin, a stack of rocks, and an extensive grape arbor are visible. The grave is seventy-five yards east of the rocks.

to load him into his car and take him to the hospital in Grangeville. On the trail, however, Bergman's condition deteriorated. When Reho reached Yellow Pine Bar, she realized her father was too sick to go farther. She got the attention of Charlie Ayres, who lived across the river on Richardson Bar. He rowed across to get them. He rowed Bergman back across the river to Richardson Bar and put him in bed in his cabin. Bergman died there on the afternoon of July 14 and was buried just east of Ayres' home, near the grave of Eugene Churchill.

Bergman's grave is marked by a simple, flat, cement stone, provided by his wife, Anna. Reho planted narcissus around the grave; they bloom each spring.

Martin Humes

The ornate obelisk erected in memory of Martin Humes has outlasted his stay on the Salmon River by a hundred years.

Humes was born in Lewis County, New York, the first child of Warren and Lucy Humes. His year of birth is uncertain because census records are inconsistent. The 1860 census, taken in Diana, New York, indicates Humes was born in 1858; in the 1900 census, Martin said 1856. It is known that Humes spent his early years near Harrisville, New York, where his father Warren owned a 630-acre farm. The farm produced maple sugar and provided well for Warren, Lucy, and their children: Martin, Elsie, Willie, Myron, Birdie, and Grant.

Additionally, Warren was involved in a resort at Waterville, New York, located in the Adirondack Mountains. Young Martin worked as a guide there. This experience led him to the West Coast.

In the 1890s, Humes arrived in the forests of northwestern Washington in Elwha River country. He earned his living as a trapper and hunting guide. He also attempted mining and listed his chief occupation as "miner" in the 1900 census.

In 1902, Humes journeyed to the Salmon River. He was a large, easy-going man and quickly made friends along the river. Robert Bailey, of Lewiston, and Clarence Harris Prescott, of Dixie, were two of his closer ones. The three men often hunted together, and Humes and Prescott worked on various placer claims together. In June 1904, Humes, Prescott, and G. B. Shelhorn located the Olympic placer claim, sixty acres on the west side of the mouth of Richardson Creek. Later Humes built a cabin at the site and spent his last days there. He also worked for the Idaho Mining Company, a firm headquartered in Seattle.

The exact cause of Humes' death is unknown. In the late fall of 1904, Humes, Bailey, and Prescott went bear hunting. They walked upriver, pulling a small wooden boat. The work was laborious, and Humes did more than his share. According to Bailey, when they arrived at Barth Hot Springs, Humes drank heavily from its waters. Shortly afterward, he became violently ill. Prescott and Bailey put him in their boat and rowed him back downstream to his cabin. For six weeks, Prescott tried to nurse him back to health, but Humes died. Although Bailey attributed it to the hot springs, others

Martin Humes' grave is on the west end of Lower Richardson Bar, past Richardson Creek, on the south side of the river. Lower Yellow Pine campsite is directly across the river from the grave.

surmised tick fever may have been the cause. Humes' obituary simply stated he died from pneumonia on Christmas Eve, 1904.

On December 26, he was buried on Lower Richardson Bar. Friends used dynamite to blast a hole in the frozen ground. At one time, his grave was surrounded by an iron fence which has since fallen away. Today only the elaborate headstone purchased by his family remains.

Jesse Root

In the heart of the Frank Church River of No Return Wilderness in Chamberlain Basin lies the legacy of Jesse Root, who grew up in the Salmon River Mountains.

He was born on March 22, 1883, in Oregon. His father, Washington Irving Root, came west from Pennsylvania. His mother was born and raised in Oregon.

What happened to Jesse's mother is unknown, but in 1891, Jesse and his father traveled to Chamberlain Basin in central Idaho, where they planned to set up a trapline and spend the winter. They were nearly killed by a freak September storm that dropped three feet of snow. They headed northeast down Chamberlain Creek, built a log cabin, and made it through the winter. This became the site of the first Root Ranch, which father and son worked for a time.

Eventually, Jesse moved south, up Chamberlain Creek to Whimstick Creek, where he built the second Root Ranch. Forest Service records indicate by 1911, Jesse had moved to the Whimstick site and filed for a homestead on March 6, 1912. He went to work for the Forest Service at this time, serving as the district ranger for the Chamberlain Basin area.

In July of 1918, Root's Whimstick Ranch was examined by Forest Supervisor Walter Mann. Root's accomplishments there in just six years were testimonial to his work ethic.

At the time, Root was living in a one-room log cabin, but he was in the process of building a new log house with two stories and six rooms. He notched and raised a log barn for hay, 30 x 30', with a pine shake roof. Additionally, he dug and rocked a double-walled root cellar. A quarter mile from his new home, Root had constructed a frame barn to hold ten tons of hay. He also built a log barn for dairy cows and a half-mile of log fence.

Root's plan was to raise cattle and cut the meadow hay that grew in the open acreage at his ranch. Annually, he put up twenty tons of hay with a mower and rake packed up to his place from the mouth of Chamberlain Creek on the Salmon River. The implements had been boated downriver from Salmon by Captain Harry Guleke.

At the time his homestead was examined by Mann, Root received notice to register in Grangeville, 150 miles northwest of his ranch, for the WWI draft. On his registration, he listed Warren, Idaho, as his permanent residence and stated that he was engaged in stock farming. He also noted that he worked as a fire guard for the Chamberlain District of the Payette National Forest. He listed his father as his nearest relative, but his father was not with him on the ranch. Blue-eyed and brown haired, Jesse stated he was "tall" and of "medium build." In the margins, the registrar wrote "physically large man."

Root returned to his ranch, remained for the next year, and on October 20, 1919, received legal title to his 157 acres. He then left and went to Warren, thirty miles to the west, to live. He opened a mercantile and ran the post office. According to the 1920 census, he was renting a house and working as the proprietor of his own general store. Over the next fifteen years, Root made a name for himself as a kind and honest man. Additionally, he worked his ranch.

In 1935 Root sold his store and headed to Salmon, fifty

Jess Root is buried near the Whitewater Campground on the Salmon River. From the east end of the campground, a trail heads east, upriver. The grave lies just north of the trailhead registration box.

miles to the east, where he planned to partner in a gold mining venture. On his way there traveling alone, he was killed for his money, and his body was dumped in the Salmon River near Kitchen Creek. Later, his body was found in an eddy by the Dale (Whitewater) Ranch, and it was buried there.

Another version of the story says Root was traveling to Salmon with Jack Reese. They had just crossed and were preparing to land on the north shore of the river near Procter

Falls, below Kitchen Creek, when their boat capsized. Reese scrambled ashore, but Root was pulled under. His body was recovered by Floyd Dale of the Dale Ranch on June 10, 1935. The Idaho County coroner ordered the body buried at the spot, forty-two miles downstream from where Root drowned.

After Root's death, his homestead was seized by Idaho County for unpaid taxes. Eventually, movie actor Wallace Beery bought it and allowed the Forest Service to build an airstrip there. The Root Ranch remains among the few private in-holdings in Chamberlain Basin.

Sam Myers

His was one of the more familiar faces in Dixie at the turn of the last century. Sometimes he drank excessively; sometimes he played cards all night. When Sam Myers died in 1921, one month shy of ninety, the Salmon River lost one of its pioneers.

Samuel Myers was born December 5, 1831, in Myerstown, Pennsylvania. His father was a farmer who worked acreage in the rolling hills of southeastern Pennsylvania.

When Myers was just nineteen, he went west for the California Gold Rush of 1849. He settled in Eldorado County, where he panned in the placer mines and earned two dollars a day. How long he remained in California is uncertain, but in the early 1860s, he returned east.

With the outbreak of the Civil War in 1861, Myers appeared in no hurry to enlist. When the Battle of Gettysburg was fought near his family home, however, it must have struck a nerve because two months later he volunteered for the Union Army.

Myers' military record reveals several discrepancies concerning his enlistment date, but in his pension papers, he asserted that he enlisted on September 1, 1863, in Indianapolis, Indiana. Private Myers served with Company H of the 115th Indiana Volunteer Infantry. At the time of his enlistment, he was five feet, seven inches, fair skinned, with blue eyes and brown hair. Before he joined the infantry, he had been working as a farmer.

As a member of the 115th, Myers saw little combat, spending most of his time on patrol and guard duty in Kentucky and Tennessee. Consequently, the 115th was disbanded in February 1864. Myers was then assigned to Company F of the 85th Indiana Volunteer Infantry and joined other Union forces on General Tecumseh Sherman's march on Atlanta, Georgia. Myers participated in the siege of Atlanta and the siege of Savannah, then fought at the Battle of Bentonville, North Carolina in March 1865. With the surrender of the Confederate forces shortly thereafter, Myers' service ended. In July of 1865, he was honorably discharged in Indianapolis.

Following the war, Myers slowly made his way west again. Immediately following his discharge, he settled in Kansas, but the plains held no attraction for him. After one year, he left. He traveled west to Trinidad, Colorado, where he remained until 1868. Then he moved to Montana, making his living as a miner. In 1881 he heard tales of gold in Idaho, and going south settled in the Wood River Valley, near present Hailey. A bit later he rode north about sixty miles to the Stanley Basin, and then eventually followed the Salmon River north and west, arriving in Elk City in 1891. With time, he came to call Dixie and the Salmon River home.

Sam worked as a miner, staking claims in the Elk City and Dixie districts. Most notable was the Eureka near Elk City, which he staked in April 1893. Also at that time he filed for a veteran's pension. In October 1896, Myers was still awaiting his pension. He reapplied, stating he was completely unable to support himself because of chronic rheumatism in both of his arms. He also suffered respiratory problems. Shortly thereafter, he began receiving his pension. Over the next twenty-five years, Myers' mining paid off and along with his monthly fifty-dollar pension, he lived comfortably.

Myers enjoyed himself. By this time, he was in his late sixties and a well-known storyteller, although a bit repetitive. He also enjoyed his whiskey. More than once, he fell from his horse in a drunken stupor on the way home and simply slept where he fell.

Although Myers could have survived on his pension, he continued to work. In 1898 he left Dixie to live on the Salmon River, where he was the first settler on what is now known as the Allison Ranch. In 1903 Myers and Ernest Sillge became partners on a forty-acre claim at the mouth of Five Mile Creek, just west downriver from the present-day Allison Ranch. The two men were good friends and worked the claim until Sillge moved eight miles farther downriver to buy Campbell's Ferry. In 1905 Myers filed a separate claim, this one for twenty

The Dixie cemetery holds the remains of many Salmon River pioneers, Sam Myers among them. The cemetery is on the south end of the town.

acres, adjacent to the Five Mile Claim. In 1910 Myers combined these two claims and filed a homestead entry.

Now in his seventies, he gave up mining to work his homestead. He cleared the land of yellow pine, built a log house and several out buildings, put up a large barn, and cultivated hay. He also raised horses. His switch from miner to farmer was noted in the 1910 census: he reported he was living free on his farm on the Salmon River. His homestead was surveyed in 1915, and the patent was granted on July

25, 1916. Myers was now eighty-four.

In June of 1921, Ernest Sillge drowned at Campbell's Ferry while crossing the river in a cable car. Myers, administrator of Sillge's estate, moved to the Ferry.

On October 19, 1921, Myers left Campbell's Ferry, bound for Dixie, on horseback. He was leading two pack horses to bring back supplies for the winter. A day later, Myers' saddle horse returned to the Ferry alone. Louis Schroeder, who had been staying with Myers at the Ferry, saddled up and rode to Dixie, expecting to find Myers somewhere along the trail, but found no sign of him. Once in Dixie, Schroeder learned that Myers had never arrived there. He and Bob Hyland then back tracked in their search.

On October 22, they found Myers' body resting on a ledge in the Salmon River Canyon, well below the pack trail. From the condition of the body, they surmised that he had been jerked from his horse by the pack horses and fell to his death. Schroeder and Hyland took the body to Dixie for burial the next day.

In addition to his sixty-one acre homestead, Myers owned: a buckboard buggy, a mowing machine and hay rake, a six-foot saw, a blacksmith outfit, three horses, and four cows with calves. In October 1922, the estate was sold to Elmer Allison of the Allison Ranch for $1,200.

Myers is buried in the Dixie cemetery. His is among the few marked graves there. Louis Larson carved the stone in 1932, and he missed the year by two. On the Salmon River, the creek that borders the east side of Allison Ranch is now known as Myers Creek, a fitting tribute.

Ella Prescott

Twice married, twice widowed, Ella Nutting Churchill Prescott found the Salmon River tested her endurance.

Ella was born in November 1855 in Dodge County, Wisconsin. Her parents, Edward and Caroline Nutting, migrated west from Vermont in the mid-1800s. Ella remained in the Wisconsin area during her early years. She met Clarence Eugene Churchill there, and they were married before a justice of the peace on March 28, 1884, in Merrill, Wisconsin. He was twenty-six; she was twenty-eight.

The couple traveled northwest to Minnesota, where Churchill worked in the iron mines of the Mesabi Range. He worked there until the late 1890s and then left for Idaho. Ella remained behind.

The 1900 census records show Ella living in Nichols, Minnesota, where she was supporting herself as a seamstress. Stella Zahn (Zand) Churchill, an adopted niece, was living with her. She was thirteen at the time. Soon after this, Ella and Stella packed up and reunited with Gene in Idaho.

Gene Churchill had established a place on Little Mallard Creek on the Salmon River. Once the two women arrived, he built a large house. Together, they created a working ranch. The result was a successful business providing food to gold miners during the boom at Thunder Mountain, fifty miles to the south. On the Three Blaze Trail from Dixie to Thunder Mountain, their home was a haven.

Life on the Salmon River took its toll, however. Robert L. Bailey, of Lewiston, who wrote the first book about the Salmon River and who eventually married Stella, wrote that

Ella was "not robust in health." Nevertheless, she endured. When Gene Churchill packed produce and fresh meat to the miners, Ella stayed behind to care for the ranch.

When Gene drowned in 1915 leaving Ella a widow, running the ranch on her own was a formidable task. Clarence Harris Prescott helped her. He had been on the river since the turn of the century and had survived the boat wreck that took Gene's life. A year later, November 4, 1916, she and Prescott were married in Elk City. At the same time, Ella filed a homestead patent on the 122-acre ranch.

Although Prescott assisted Ella on the ranch, his health was poor. He suffered from the after-effects of a gunshot wound received in 1912 when he was shot by a friend who mistook him for a bear. Periodically, Prescott sought medical care in town. In November 1920, on one such trip to Newsome, he contracted pneumonia and died. He is buried in Kooskia.

With the homestead entry pending, Ella refused to leave the Churchill Ranch, yet her own failing health made caring for the place impossible. Joseph Arthur Hoover, who arrived shortly after Prescott's death, did the chores for her. Ella's sister, Bertie Lyons, also came to the river to care for her.

Ella received title to her homestead in February 1922. At this time Ella made a will, leaving her entire estate in equal shares to Hoover and Lyons. Ella died in October of that year. In addition to the ranch, her estate included $102.

Hoover and Lyons buried Ella at the west end of the ranch near Little Mallard Creek. They placed a large boulder over the top of her grave. Today, it is protected by a pole fence, fifty yards southeast of the Little Mallard Creek generator.

Joe Hoover married Bertie, then sold the Churchill Ranch in 1930 for $2,500. It is now known as the Whitewater Ranch.

Rose Cook

Every grave tells a story. This is the story of Rose Cook.

Born in Salem, Oregon, in December 1862, Rose Bernardi Aiken Cook was the second daughter of Joseph Bernardi and Rosalia Gipherd Bernardi. Joseph immigrated to the United States from Switzerland; Rosalia came from Germany. When and where they first met is unknown. They settled first in California, then moved to Salem, where Joseph made a living as a liquor dealer. A Catholic family, they had eight children, five girls and three boys.

When daughter Rose was seventeen, she married Joseph Aiken, whose family was among the early settlers of the Willamette Valley in Oregon. They married on June 25, 1881, at her father's home in Salem. At the time, Joseph was twenty-eight years old.

Rose and Joseph remained in the Salem area, where he made a living as a bartender. Both were listed in the 1895 census. Rose described herself as five feet, three inches tall, 130 pounds, with dark skin. Her husband stood five feet, nine inches and weighed 176 pounds, with a light complexion. They had no children at that time.

Joseph Aiken died on April 19, 1900, and was buried in the Salem Pioneer Cemetery. Rose then moved in with her mother, who by that time was also a widow. Jake Bernardi, a plumber and Rose's youngest brother, supported the family. Shortly thereafter, Rose left Salem for Idaho.

What brought her to Idaho is unknown now. Some time before 1903, Rose arrived in Elk City, a primitive mining camp, where she went to work as the school teacher. She caught the eye of Elk City postmaster, Warren Cook. He was a handsome, hard-working young man and before long, he proposed. The couple was married by a justice of the peace in Grangeville on June 22, 1903. Rose was forty years old; Warren, twenty-seven. The next day, they took the stage back to Elk City and began their new life together.

Cook heard that Campbell's Ferry on the Salmon River was for sale. The ferry connected the Dixie-Gospel Hump area with the Thunder Mountain mines. Thinking it might be a lucrative business opportunity, he bought the property from C. E. Churchill, and he and his wife moved to the river.

Newspaper reports indicate that Rose and Warren were well respected, and Rose, in particular, was "favorably known." She told friends that after her marriage to Warren, her life was "ideal."

In the spring of 1905, at age forty-two, Rose became pregnant. In early October, she became ill, stricken with what was then known as "apoplexy," most likely a stroke. Immediately afterward, Jim Moore, their neighbor from across the river arrived to help, as did Ella Churchill, from the Churchill Ranch, who served as midwife. Despite their assistance, Rose was unable to deliver the baby. Moore later told the story. "First we prayed that she would have the baby.

Then we prayed for it to be over soon."

The baby was stillborn. Shortly after, on the evening of October 12, 1905, Rose died.

She and her child were buried two days later above the meadow at Campbell's Ferry. People from Elk City and Dixie made the ten-mile trip to the Ferry for the funeral.

Rose's death was devastating for Warren. While no record exists to substantiate it, a Cook family legend asserts that Rose had a young child, a son, before she married Warren.

Rose Aiken Cook is buried at Campbell's Ferry, approximately sixty yards southeast of the old cabin. Her wooden marker was made by Cort Conley.

Allegedly, shortly after Rose's death, Warren left Campbell's Ferry accompanied by the young boy. Where they went or what they did is a mystery now, but perhaps Warren left him with a family in Lewiston, with the understanding that the boy not be told the name of his birth parents.

Warren himself never spoke of the matter. He even refused to discuss Rose with his own family. Eventually, he raised another family with his second wife, Helga Peterson, whom he married in 1908. In 1951, when Warren died, Peterson was compelled to prove in probate court that Rose and her child had died in childbirth, and that Warren had no other heirs.

In Oregon the 1900 census indicated Rose was a widow and childless. In Rose's obituary, carried in the *Elk City News*, no son was listed among her survivors. If Rose did have a son, his identity remains a secret.

Norman Wolfe

Children who came with their families to live on the Salmon River were warned repeatedly about its dangers. While the river was inviting with its fishing, swimming, and exploring, it also was to be feared.

Norman Wolfe, born August 5, 1940, was the first son of George and Reho Wolfe. In 1944, George and Reho left Montana for a life on the Salmon River, taking Norman with them. They spent their first year at the Crofoot Ranch, one mile north of the Salmon River, up Rattlesnake Creek. In 1945 the family moved down to the river, staying at the Allison

Ranch, four miles west. There George helped Elmer Allison rebuild his house, which had burned a year earlier.

In early June of 1945, Reho's father, John Bergman, made his way to the river for an extended stay with his daughter. He arrived before his luggage did.

On June 29, George and Norman, along with two pack horses, walked southwest downriver to the Dale Ranch to retrieve Bergman's luggage, a distance of five miles. On their way down river, they stopped at Charlie Ayres' place on Richardson Bar to catch up on the latest river news. Charlie was entertaining his nephew and invited Norman to stay while his dad went on to the Dale Ranch. Then George could pick up Norman on the way home. Norman, however, refused, and the two traveled on down the river.

In June the water on the Salmon River and its tributaries runs high, and this June was typical. On the return trip, George and Norman made their way carefully up the trail, George leading the pack horses loaded with Bergman's belongings. When they reached Big Mallard Creek, George told Norman to wait while he led the horses across the swollen stream. Once he had the horses safely across, he would return for Norman.

But instead of waiting, Norman attempted to follow by crossing on a log bridge that spanned the creek. It was slippery, and he lost his footing and fell into the torrent. George frantically scrambled down the streambank racing the water, lunging into the stream, where momentarily he managed to grab Norman's hand. Then the current sucked him away into the Salmon River and out of sight.

Norman Wolfe's grave is hidden among the pines at Campbell's Ferry. Located on the old ferry trail upstream from the Campbell's Ferry Bridge, it is nestled between two pine trees, approximately 200 yards north of the old cabins.

Anguished, cold, wet, and now hampered by a sprained ankle, George limped back up the river to tell his wife. He had nightmares for years, and later he told his other children, "It's the worst thing in the world to have ahold of your son and have him slip away." For George and Reho, life was never the same because George never got over what happened, and she blamed him for the accident.

The family and friends along the river spent the next weeks searching the banks of the river. Then, in late afternoon on

July 19, Norman's body was discovered by Emmett Davis in an eddy below Campbell's Ferry. Residents at the Ferry retrieved it, and Frances Zaunmiller and others buried the boy. The next day, she walked three miles up river to the Dale Ranch to inform the Wolfes. Reputedly, Reho resented Frances for burying Norman without her. However Reho in her later years told a different story. She stated she was in Elk City when she received a telephone call from Zaunmiller, who told her of the discovery. Immediately, she made the thirty mile trip south to Campbell's Ferry, and she, along with other residents of the Ferry, buried Norman by the moonlight.

A 4 x 8" aluminum marker made by David Wolfe, a brother Norman never knew, now marks the grave. It is located just above the old Ferry trail at Campbell's Ferry.

Reho Wolfe planted bearded irises at the mouth of Big Mallard Creek where her son was last seen. The flowers, a gentle reminder, still bloom in spring.

Jim Moore

Master craftsman, rancher, miner, moonshiner, story-teller—as a legend on the Salmon River, Jim Moore combined them all.

Moore came west from Kentucky in 1883 and found his way to the Salmon River in 1898. According to his account, he came to the river to hide and save himself from hanging after getting involved in outlaw activities on the West Coast.

Once on the river, he had no desire to leave.

In the 1900 census, Moore said he had been born in Indiana in August 1866. Other sources state his birth date as August 20, 1867, in Carmine, Illinois. On occasion, Moore told a different story. He claimed his birth date was unknown because he was an orphan. He said that at a young age he had run away to escape an abusive foster father. His flight took him west, where he sought fortune and finally drifted down into the Salmon River Canyon.

When he first arrived on the river, he lived with William Campbell at Campbell's Ferry. In his census papers he wrote that he was Campbell's servant and farm laborer. At the time, he was well on his way to establishing his own place on the bar just west across the river from Campbell's Ferry.

In 1898 Moore, along with C. E. Churchill, constructed a log cabin that was to become Moore's home, the first building on the bar. For the next fifteen years, Moore, working mostly by himself, completed eight more structures, including a two-story barn, four bunkhouses, a tool shed, a chicken coop, and a root cellar. Aside from the root cellar, all the buildings had rock foundations and were built of Ponderosa pine shaped with a cross-cut saw, a broad ax, and an adz. They were the best crafted structures on the river at that time.

Moore's industriousness was not limited to his carpentry. In September 1900, he filed a claim on the property, naming it the Slide Creek Placer. He held the claim for the next forty years. His interest, however, lay largely in his garden and orchard, and he cleared the bar for hay as well. He built a wooden flume over 800 feet long from Slide Creek to bring water to the hay. He dug 1,800 feet of irrigation ditch around and through the bar to take care of his garden and orchard.

During the mining boom at Thunder Mountain, fifty-three miles to the south, Moore's place was a waystation for weary miners and freighters on the Three Blaze Trail. Moore sold them fruits, vegetables, eggs, beef, and lodging. Between 1900 and 1902, the height of the boom, Moore said he served over 1,800 miners.

He also grew a large crop of corn from which he made moonshine; he kept his still hidden in the hills north of his cabin. He also made apple jack from his orchard each fall. He combined apples, crab apples, and sugar and let them ferment. When the mixture was ready, he drew off a gallon jug and then buried it in the snow for the night. The water and pulp froze, but not the alcohol. He poured off the alcohol and sold the concoction to the miners.

Once the mining rush was over, Moore was left in peace to work his garden and tend his orchard. A fine craftsman, he built furniture from hand-carved wood and tanned hides. He made a retreat for himself on the river and during the last twenty years of his life, never ventured farther than Dixie, twenty miles northwest by trail. Although isolated, Moore kept himself attuned to the outside world. He was an avid reader—his cabin walls were lined with books—and he followed the politics of the day. He maintained a battery-operated radio on his kitchen table. In his later years, travelers along the Salmon River found Moore sitting on his front porch where he watched for the people who traveled the river. He did not go out of his way to be friendly, but was

From the Campbell's Ferry Pack Bridge, a good trail leads west to Jim Moore's place on the north side of the river. Moore is buried just north of the cabins he built on the bar. A well-worn trail leads to the grave.

known to share his homemade wine and pear brandy with strangers, if he liked them.

In the final years of his life, Moore became close friends with Frances and Joe Zaunmiller, who lived across the river at Campbell's Ferry.

In spring 1942, Moore became too ill to care for himself. The Zaunmillers moved him to their cabin. On April 25, 1942, Moore died. Knowing he did not want to leave the river, the Zaunmillers, along with Bert Rhodes and Doralita Pratt, wrapped Moore's body in a canvas mule pack and ferried him across the river to his place. They buried him on the hillside above his cabin. The Zaunmillers then notified Idaho County Sheriff by telephone.

Moore never filed a homestead application on the bar, only a mining claim. This claim was passed on to several people, including Frances Zaunmiller and Bert Rhodes. In 1966, after several court battles, the claim was voided, and the site reverted to public land.

The Forest Service maintains Jim Moore's place and has restored two of the buildings. In 1978 the cabins became part of the National Register of Historic Places.

Eric Blaine Lym

Eric Lym, who died at age thirty-three, was born on July 14, 1962, in Portland, Oregon, the second son of Bonnie and Bob Ford. Bonnie divorced Ford and married Bob Lym, who cared for Eric as though he were his own son.

As a child, Eric was known for his sense of humor, which often led him into mischief. At home, he was forever sneaking into the kitchen to untie his mother's apron. At school, he refused to let learning interfere with his cheery outlook. Above all, Eric loved the outdoors, especially fishing. A picture of him at age nine shows him in waders, carrying a rod with a sizable fish on the end of his line and a smile nearly as long.

On the Fourth of July in 1972, Eric and his family were

with friends on the Columbia River searching for arrowheads. He was riding in the back of an open jeep on a rough road and fell out, landing on his head.

Rushed to the hospital, he lay in a coma for ten days. Doctors told the Lyms there was no hope of recovery. But Bonnie Lym refused to give up. After forty days, Eric regained consciousness, but his brain stem suffered severe damage. He was paralyzed on his right side and blind in his right eye. Talking and walking had to be relearned. After years of support, and despite a spastic left hand and a crooked gait, eventually Eric was able to proceed with his life.

In 1973 the Lyms moved to Riggins and Eric enrolled in school, but it was difficult for him. While he struggled with his physical problems, other students often made fun of him. He persevered, nonetheless, and graduated in 1980.

Eric matured physically, but not emotionally. After the accident, he tended to see life like a nine-year-old. When people were dishonest or mistreated him, he responded like a child—with predictable consequences.

Unable to live independently, Eric remained at home. Particularly close to his grandparents, he chopped their firewood and did their chores. When his grandfather died, he moved in with his grandmother for a time, taking care of her and doing all the chores she could not. His helpfulness was well known throughout Riggins. He chopped and stacked firewood for many elderly widows.

Frustrations with his physical limitations and social difficulties led Eric to drink. In early spring of 1991, Eric's personal problems were nearly unmanageable; he needed help. Reho Wolfe, a longtime friend of Eric's grandmother, suggested that a summer on the Salmon River might be the answer. As soon as the ice left the river, he traveled to Rhett Creek, where he lived in a small cabin at Wolfe's place. He earned his keep there by clearing brush, irrigating her garden, and otherwise serving as a general caretaker.

Wolfe became his mentor. Most important, she introduced him to the art of hitching rides on jet boats. She also taught him how little in the way of possessions was required to survive on the river.

Eric toughened. Although small, he grew stronger, and he could now hike the steep trails of the Salmon with ease. He wore a thick black beard and a full head of hair. His abnormal gait and speech were still evident, but river people accepted him in a way urban people did not. He lived a life many people envied. He found a certain peace on the river.

Lym stayed with Wolfe for two summers. Then he decided to move to Campbell's Ferry, where he would be truly independent for the first time. He wrote to Joe Denton, one of three owners of Campbell's Ferry. Lym asked if he could live at the Ferry as a caretaker. Denton did not respond immediately, so Lym hitched his way to the Ferry and waited for Denton to fly in, in order to ask him for the job. Denton agreed.

Lym lived at Campbell's Ferry for two years. During that time, he and his German Shepherd, Sam, became familiar figures to boaters who visited the Ferry to see it and the historic Jim Moore site across the river.

During his second summer at Campbell's Ferry, Lym began

to take a more noticeable interest in the raft parties floating the river. He watched for them, and when they neared the Campbell's Ferry Bridge, he would leap from it into the river, fifty feet below. When Denton learned of Lym's stunt, he told him it must stop. Lym ignored him. Since Denton had liability concerns, he terminated their agreement. The following summer, Lym was back at Rhett Creek.

In August 1995, while at Rhett Creek, Lym learned that several of his friends were rafting the river. He decided to hike up to Campbell's Ferry and surprise them with a leap from the bridge. On the afternoon of August 6, 1995, he hiked 5 miles to the Ferry. There he met Denton and his family, had dinner with them, and then camped beneath the bridge awaiting his friends.

They arrived the next day and Lym urged them to leap with him. All declined, but he was undeterred; it was his first jump of the season, the fortieth of his life. He made the leap in full view, friends watching from a beach immediately downstream. They saw him hit the water and surface and immediately knew something was wrong. Before anyone could go to his rescue, however, he was swept through the rapids downstream and disappeared.

A week later, Lym's body was found at China Bar, four miles downstream, by a rafting party. His parents considered burying him at Rhett Creek but decided instead to bury him near their home on the banks of the Little Salmon River near Riggins, one-quarter mile from the main Salmon.

Although Lym's fall from the jeep affected him physically and emotionally, his mind was unusually astute. In his

Eric Lym is buried in his parent's garden near the family home on the Little Salmon River, a half-mile south of where it empties into the Main Salmon.

thirties, he took to writing poetry as a way of coping with his difficulties. In a poem found in his cabin at Rhett Creek, Lym wrote: "May no one be less good for having come within my influence."

Robert Hemminger

Robert Hemminger was a hunter who could not resist the abundant game that roamed the numerous canyons of the Salmon River.

He was born around 1914, the son of W. H. Hemminger, a rancher from Wildhorse, Idaho, on the middle Snake River. The young Hemminger grew up in the area and was well known to people in nearby Council Valley.

In the fall of 1936, he left the familiar Snake River country to hunt in the Salmon River drainage near Dixie. No one knows how long he planned to be there. One account says Hemminger was on a hunting trip. Another states that Hemminger was planning to winter in a cabin on Ruff Creek, fourteen miles southeast of Dixie. He had permission from the owner, Rex Coppernoll of Lewiston.

On the morning of November 21, 1936, Hemminger left Dixie. When Hemminger's father had not heard from him for two weeks, he went to Dixie, where he organized a search party. Aided by a deputy sheriff from Dixie and using a tractor, the elder Hemminger and the search party headed south to the river.

According to reports in the *Idaho County Free Press*, the group found Robert Hemminger's body near the trail on a slope above the river. As he walked, he slipped on ice and fell over a thousand feet. The shattered body was recovered December 16. Rather than pack it out on a horse, the group buried Hemminger where they found him.

Another version of Hemminger's death says that he was hunting for mountain sheep on the steep banks of the canyon between Ruff Creek and Fall Creek. He shot a ram, and as he went to retrieve it, he slipped on the icy slope and, unable to walk, eventually froze to death.

Hemminger's remains now rest in the river canyon. Forest Service records reveal the grave was located at the head of a draw between Ruff Creek and Fall Creek. It was marked in the 1930s and again in 1977.

Reho Wolfe

Demanding, overbearing, high-spirited, resourceful—all describe Reho Wolfe, who had a fifty-six year relationship with the Salmon River.

Reho was born in Denio, Oregon, on April 18, 1916, the youngest child of John and Anne Ferdland Bergman. Reho's father was a frequent gambler most and an infrequent farmer. It was a destructive combination, and the family was forced to move many times during her young life. Her mother, Anne, raised the Bergman brood, which also included Arthur, Burton, Viva, and Alga.

These early struggles gave Reho her indomitable spirit; throughout her life she rose to every challenge and surmounted most. Blessed with a good mind, she did well in school and graduated from Kamiah High School in 1935 as class salutatorian. She used her formal education all her life.

On March 8, 1936, Reho married George Wolfe, a trained musician. They had their first child, Norman, in 1940 while living in Moscow. From there, they moved to Missoula, Montana, where George taught music at the National Institute of Art and Music. Life was good for the young couple until the outbreak of World War II. While George was too old for the regular draft, the wartime draft was a different story. George had no intention of going to war, so he and Reho loaded up Norman and a few belongings and headed to Idaho and the wilderness of the Salmon River.

The specific circumstances of how and why the Wolfes ended up where they did is unclear, but in the winter of 1944, Reho, George, and Norman moved to the Crofoot Ranch, one mile north of the Salmon River, up Rattlesnake Creek, having come from Montana through the MacGruder Corridor. George was familiar with the area, having worked for the Forest Service for a time. They stayed at the ranch for one year before heading down to the Salmon River. Once on the river, they moved in with Elmer Allison at the Allison Ranch. George helped Elmer build a new cabin. Reho and George also became parents again when daughter Carol was born.

In the spring of 1945, John Bergman, critically ill, came to the river to live with Reho. His belongings were delivered to the Dale (Whitewater) Ranch, and George and Norman went to retrieve them. On the journey home, Norman fell into Big Mallard Creek and was swept away. Two weeks later, John Bergman died.

The tragedy overwhelmed Reho. The Wolfes, with Carol in tow, left the river and settled in Lewiston, Idaho. George taught music lessons there and worked as a railroad storekeeper. Reho was busy raising the family. They had six more children: Sharon, David, Marge, Linda, John, and Billy.

With the growing family, George worked long hours and multiple jobs, and Reho took domestic employment. George became ill with hepatitis, and before long, the entire family was infected. The children fell behind in school and with their parents working so hard, they had little supervision.

Reho felt best when the family was on the Salmon River each summer. They stayed at an abandoned cabin on Gaines Bar near Rhett Creek. Monroe Hancock, an old friend who lived on the river, suggested Reho file a mining claim on the site. After the couple discussed the matter, Reho filed the Billie placer claim in August 1958. They withdrew the children from school, packed their belongings and a considerable number of supplies, and left for the river.

Idaho, like all states, had a compulsory education law, and according to the Idaho County School District, Reho Wolfe was in violation of that law. On October 8, a warrant for her arrest was issued on grounds she was "contributing to the delinquency of minors and causing their habitual truancy."

Reho was unruffled. Using Calvert School correspondence courses, the children had their lessons every weekday from 8:30 a.m. to 3:30 p.m. After hours, they learned more practical lessons about survival. For Reho, that would be the key to her children's success. In the summer of 1959, she told a *Cosmopolitan* reporter, "I want my children to learn more than textbooks can offer."

Reho continued to teach her children on the river, and Grangeville school officials continued to grouse about it. But Idaho County Prosecuting Attorney Wayne MacGregor, Jr.,

Reho Wolfe is buried on Gaines Bar, on the north side of the river, directly across from China Bar. Her grave is located in an open field, approximately 100 yards west of her cabin.

was not certain that the Wolfe children were not receiving a proper or legal education. Rather than serve the arrest warrant, he held it until he could be advised by Idaho's Attorney General, Graydon Smith. The two of them convinced the Idaho County School Board that since Reho was teaching the children, she was not in violation of the law. At the end of October, the charge against Reho was dropped.

In the middle of home schooling, Reho faced another fight.

Forest Service officials questioned the legitimacy of the Wolfe claim and performed a mineral assay in October 1958 to determine whether or not it was valid. The Forest Service then denied the Billie Placer claim on Gaines Bar. Reho, however, appealed the decision. In May of 1959, she walked twenty-seven miles from the river to the Red River Ranger Station to defend her claim. It was eventually reinstated in 1960 by the Secretary of the Interior. In order to keep the claim, Reho and George had to post a $3,000 reclamation bond. Reho resisted. The haggling between the Wolfes and the Forest Service continued for thirty years. In 1965 the Forest Service granted the Wolfes a special-use permit to retain the cabins on Gaines Bar. In 1987 Reho finally reached an agreement with the Forest Service: she gave up her title claim to the cabin on Gaines Bar in return for the right to use it for the rest of her life.

The struggle with the Forest Service and Idaho County School Board were evidence of Reho's determination. After one year of home schooling the children on the Salmon River, she returned to Lewiston. She enrolled in Lewis-Clark Normal School there and earned a teaching degree. Then she packed up her children and moved to Troy, Montana, where she taught first grade for one year. Once again, she returned to Lewiston

This was a pattern: Reho was constantly on the go, changing locations or jobs. For a time she worked as a cook, first at the hospital in Medical Lake, Washington; then at Mackay Bar and the Stonebreaker Ranch in the Salmon River Canyon. Even in her later years, she moved often. According to her son John, Reho sometimes went to Gaines Bar one day and headed home to Lewiston the next.

Reho wanted to be on the river every summer, and she took the children with her. She taught them how to survive on next to nothing. She laid out three gardens on there, two on the lower field and one next to the house. She grew everything the family needed. Each breakfast she served the children fresh trout, bacon, and pancakes. For dinner they might have bear, deer, or snake—whatever was at hand with gunshot. She became an expert with medicinal herbs, treating her illnesses and those of others.

While Reho is remembered as a resourceful, enlightened woman, she could also be difficult and demanding. When the couple divorced, the children drifted off to their own homes and lives. Still, Reho held fast to the river. She hitched jet boat rides with outfitters who dropped her off at her cabin. She was befriended by the people on the river—those at Shepp Ranch, Mackay Bar, Yellow Pine Bar, and China Bar. She and Frances Wisner of Campbell's Ferry became the old-timers on the river, until Frances's death in 1986; Reho was the last.

In her later years, Reho's health began to fail. She was diagnosed with a heart problem, but refused to take medication. She preferred her herbs, especially arnica. She only took her prescription drugs if she was feeling terrible.

One late evening in February of 1998, John Wolfe received a phone call from his mother: she wanted to go to the river. John told her he would take her as soon as he could. But Reho could not wait. That night she got in her car and drove to the river. She planned to be at the end of the Salmon River Road twenty-six miles east of Riggins in the morning to catch a jet boat ride. Outside of Riggins, she fell asleep at the wheel and ran off the road. Wolfe broke both legs and suffered numerous other injuries.

She spent the spring of 1998 in Lewiston recuperating, but insisted on returning to her home in the Salmon River Canyon. In June, with the help of her children, she made her way to the river even though she was still unable to walk on her own. According to Joyce Close, who lived on China Bar, across the river from Gaines Bar, Reho was revitalized when she arrived back on the river. By July 1, she felt well enough to mow the grass. She pushed the mower about twenty-five feet, then sat down and had a beer with her son John. She died during the night.

The river community (sixty-six people) gathered for her funeral. The Forest Service granted special permission for her burial at Gaines Bar, where her grave is now marked with an inscribed stone.

Jack Rainger

Many young men traveled to the Salmon River to earn their fortunes. While most worked placer claims, a few, like Jack Rainger (Ranger), dreamed of a different life.

Early information on Rainger is unclear, although in the early 1900s, several families by that name lived in northern Idaho. Jack Rainger was in Grangeville in the early 1920s, and in 1924 he was working for the Nez Perce National Forest.

Shortly thereafter—May 1926—Rainger was on the river, where he located a mining claim on Boise Bar, about three miles upstream from the Painter Mine. He named it the Boise Bar placer claim, and it included twenty acres. But by midsummer of 1926, Rainger had changed his mind about mining the site and decided his fortune lay in another endeavor.

Rainger and a partner named Partridge decided to build and operate a hunting and fishing resort at Boise Bar: the Gameland Sporting Ranch. Both of them would guide their guests to the best hunting and fishing on the river.

The partners spent the summer of 1926 clearing Boise Bar and erecting a 16 x 40′ log structure used as their main lodge and dining hall. Guests were to be warmed with a four-foot wide open fireplace. Three sides of the lodge opened onto an eight-foot wide covered deck. Additionally, Rainger and Partridge planned a three-acre garden for the following summer in order to provide their guests with fresh vegetables.

On August 5, an article in the *Idaho County Free Press* announced that the guest ranch was open. Rainger and Partridge offered special prices to Idaho County residents as a local introduction to their services. No one had an opportunity to take the offer, because within a week, Rainger was dead. The cause of his death is a mystery.

Most accounts attribute Rainger's death to his lack of experience. On August 7, 1926, witnesses reported that Rainger saw a mountain sheep on the opposite side of the

The weathered headboard of Jack Rainger sits just above the high-water mark on the north side of the Salmon River, immediately west of Teepee Creek. It is visible from the river.

river, shot it, and then swam the river fully clothed in an attempt to retrieve it. He drowned. His body surfaced a few days later at the mouth of Teepee Creek, and he was buried there.

Old-timers on the river, however, told a more sinister tale. They portrayed Rainger and Partridge as disreputable, stealing from others who lived along the river. Both Rainger and Partridge were killed, each shot in the head, as retribution. What happened to the body of Partridge is unknown, but Rainger is buried at Teepee Creek along with his dream.

John Painter

When John R. Painter showed up on the Salmon River, everyone noticed. He developed the first hunting lodge on the river, as well as one of the larger mines.

Painter was born in Centerville, Maryland, on October 12, 1861. He was raised in Philadelphia, Pennsylvania, where he married Mary, two years older than he. The couple had four children in Pennsylvania, three of whom survived to adulthood: Mary, Marguerite, and William.

In the early 1890s, Painter moved his family to Wyoming and remained there for the next eighteen years. He raised stock, ranched, and mined in Bighorn and Park counties. His name endures with Painter Mine and Painter Gulch, both in Park County, located near the Wyoming-Montana border.

Painter made his first trip to Idaho County in 1908, arriving in Elk City. He staked a claim there, the Neversweat, on January 1, 1909. Later that year, he made his way to the Salmon River, where on August 21, 1909, he purchased the Jersey Placer Claims 1 and 2 from Joseph Eakin. He paid one dollar for them.

Painter returned to Wyoming in 1910, but his heart was not there. In 1911 he abandoned his wife and children and returned to the Salmon River. His arrival was the source of much speculation in Salmon City, for he appeared to be wealthy. On May 11, 1911, with Captain Guleke as his guide, he loaded a fleet of boats with mining supplies, including a generator, and headed for his Jersey Claims.

In addition to his mining endeavors, Painter also built the first hunting lodge on the river, which he called "The

Bungalow." Outfitted with fine furnishings, it included an elaborate wooden bar, mirrors, and a pool table. A large rock fireplace was a focal point. It is all that remains of the lodge today.

Even though Painter reputedly was in the mining business, he made some efforts at ranching. In April 1917, he applied for a homestead, thirty-four acres at Jersey Creek Bar. That application was granted in October 1929.

In 1919 Painter staked the sites for which he is best known, the Surprise Lode claims. Six in all, they are located on the south side of the river running from Little Five Mile Creek to Five Mile Creek. His elaborate operation included a water-powered two-stamp mill. Remnants of his efforts can still be seen along both banks of the river.

By 1920 it was obvious that Painter was an Idaho resident. For the first time he appeared in the Idaho census and stated that he farmed for a living. He confirmed that he was still married; however, the woman living with him was Ellen Jones, his housekeeper.

For the next fifteen years, Painter lived a life of both industry and indolence. The Bungalow burned in 1922; he built a new house on the downstream side of Jersey Creek. He worked his claims and raised cattle, although he sold his entire herd in 1924. His son, William, still of Wyoming, often came to the river to help him with the mine.

In May of 1934, Painter began to order his affairs. He made a list of all the bills he owed: $2,000 to Ellen Jones for wages from 1917 to 1922 and from June 1931 to May 1934; $525 to L.R. Powelson's store for supplies such as tobacco, butter, and bacon; $97 to Alexander and Freidenrich General Store for a razor, toothpaste, shoes and socks, witch hazel, and a box of 12-gauge shotgun shells. In all, his debts totaled $2,702.

A little less than a year later, Painter and his housekeeper, Ellen Jones, traveled to Grangeville, where they were married by a justice of the peace on March 14, 1935. Painter was seventy-four years old. Then in June 1935, Painter wrote his will, instructing his administrator Wilbur Campbell to pay all of his debts, including funeral expenses. What was left

John Painter's grave can be found on the east side of Jersey Creek across from the Painter Mine. It is situated just northwest of a large rock chimney, all that remains of his hunting lodge.

over was to be given to his surviving children, William and Marguerite, and a grandson, George Heald, all of whom lived in Wyoming. Painter valued his estate at $35,000: his homestead, the Surprise Group quartz claims, the Painter millsite, and the Surprise Group millsite.

John Painter died of a heart attack on August 27 the following year. His death made front-page news in the *Idaho County Free Press*. He was buried the next day on his homestead, with residents from both Elk City and Dixie riding down to his funeral.

Wilbur Campbell began the probate process, but Ellen Jones Painter wasted no time in challenging the will. In court documents filed one month after her husband's death, she declared her marriage voided the will, and she asked that she be made administrator of the estate. When Painter's children failed to object, the court granted her request.

Ellen Painter discovered her husband's affairs were not completely in order. She paid most of his remaining bills, including the one to herself for $2,000. She gave herself an additional $644 for services performed between May 1934 and the day of her marriage. The largest creditors Ellen faced, however, were W. M. Wilson and H. A. Wilson of Seattle, who demanded $11,298 from the estate. Painter had transactions with the Wilsons regarding lease-purchase options on the Surprise Mine but defaulted on his obligation. After three years of negotiations, the Wilsons settled the claim for $600.

In 1939 Ellen Painter sold the entire property to Gordon Prentice for $15,000, and he continued to work the mine until

1953. Since then there have been several owners. In 1994, the Forest Service acquired the Painter homestead on the north side of the river. The south side remains in private hands, an in-holding within the Frank Church River of No Return Wilderness.

Sylvan Hart

He was the subject of a *Sports Illustrated* piece and at least fifty newspaper articles. On the river he was known as an eccentric, a hermit, a genius, a philosopher. He was all of those things and more. Sylvan Ambrose Hart, also known as "Buckskin Bill," remains one of the most recognized names on the Salmon River.

Hart was one of six children born to Oliver (Artie) and Malissa Hart in Oklahoma in 1906. His father supported the family by farming. He also raised horses for racing and betting. Malissa did not approve and eventually left Artie.

At an early age, Hart was educated in a one-room school house where he said he learned everything he needed to know. He learned to read, which developed into a life-long love for books. He eventually went on to college, attending three before earning a degree in English literature at the University of Oklahoma.

After one year at graduate school, where he studied petroleum engineering, he quit and traveled to Idaho. He arrived in Idaho City first and tried placer mining. Then in the fall of 1931, he traveled north to Moscow and enrolled at the University of Idaho. After one semester, Hart left for the Salmon River and Five Mile Bar. It was his home for the rest of his life.

At first, Sylvan's father lived with him. They moved into an old cabin, raised a huge garden, and did their best to survive the Depression, growing tobacco, which could be used to barter for other necessities. Artie soon left.

Over the next ten years, Sylvan cleared the land and cultivated a garden. He hunted, fished, observed the wildlife, and learned the intricacies of the river. During this time he earned his nickname "Buckskin Bill." According to Hart, one day he made his way to Mackay Bar, three miles downstream, wearing a handmade deerskin coat. Don Oberbillig, whose brother John owned Mackay Bar, took one look at Sylvan and christened him "Buckskin Bill." The name stuck.

With the outbreak of World War II, Hart decided he should serve his country. He walked to Dixie, then hitched a ride to Grangeville, where he visited the Army recruiter. However, he flunked his physical. Still, wanting to make a contribution, he traveled to Kansas and went to work at the Boeing plant as a toolmaker. Eventually the Army accepted him. He was stationed in the Aleutian Islands for a short time, but saw no combat there. Sent to Texas, he was promoted to sergeant and worked on the Norden bombsight. Once the war was over, Hart was discharged, and he returned to Idaho and Five Mile Bar.

For the next twenty years, Sylvan lived in secluded anonymity. He did seasonal jobs for the Forest Service, working on lookouts and clearing trails. Sometimes he guided for Mackay Bar. Most of the time, however, he worked on his own place and pursued his interests. He added three structures at Five Mile Bar—all still stand. He enlarged his garden, and he built a catwalk along a steep rock cliff just west of Five Mile Bar. It permitted him to walk down to Mackay Bar even if the river was high.

Firearms fascinated him. He made flintlock rifles; one required over a year to complete. He also carved knives with intricate detail and sold some of them. He made his own cooking utensils and fashioned his own clothes from the skins of animals he killed. Many of his weapons and tools are on display at St. Gertrude's Museum in Cottonwood, Idaho.

Hart received a veteran's pension but often failed to cash the checks. When he did, he spent the money on items he could not make himself. Each fall he headed to town: Grangeville, Boise, McCall. He purchased enough supplies to last through the winters spent on the river. His purchases always included tea, sugar, flannel shirts, and wool pants, his usual attire, especially on trips out of the canyon.

In the late 1960s, his life changed dramatically when a young writer published an article in *Sports Illustrated* about him titled "Last of the Mountain Men." Hart became a celebrity. He began receiving cards and letters, and in the summers hundreds of visitors made their way to Five Mile Bar. Rodney Cox, Hart's nephew, also arrived with his wife and stayed for the next seven years.

Hart greeted boatloads of tourists who stopped at his place. He dressed up in his buckskin or bearskin outfits, putting on one of his leather hats. By the summer of 1974, Cox initiated a visitation charge for outfitters who stopped with their clients.

In the fall of 1975, Cox's influence ended. His oldest son, Jeremiah, was accidentally killed. After his son's death, Cox left the river with his wife and their other two children.

But Hart could never escape his notoriety. He obliged the visitors who stopped. His trips out of the canyon became more frequent, and when he visited Boise, he always made the front-page. He spoke to Idaho school children, exhibited his handiwork, and told his tales. He even traveled to Iceland and Russia. During the winter, however, he returned to the Salmon River and its isolation.

Sylvan Hart is buried directly west of the cabin he used as his winter sleeping quarters.

Although Hart squatted on Five Mile Bar for over twenty years, he eventually purchased a mining claim to part of it. In July 1967, he bought 4.5 acres of the Blackfoot mining claim, also known as the Painter mill site, from Martin and Opal Fuhling of Stanwood, Washington. It had been patented by Gordon Prentice in 1946, converting it to private property.

With his own land, Buckskin grew old beside the Salmon River. He welcomed weekly visits from the crew at Mackay Bar who delivered his mail. On April 29, 1980, three men from there stopped with his delivery. When Hart did not greet them at the river's edge, they went to check on him. They found him in his cabin, pale and too weak to get his glycerin tablets. They gave him his medicine and in a short time, he perked up. The men promised to check back that evening. As they left, he told them that when they returned, "I'll either be feeling better or dead."

The men returned that evening and found him dead, sitting in his favorite chair in front of the hearth, dressed in his best wool suit.

Hart's body was taken to Grangeville for a funeral service, but it was his expressed desire to be buried on the river. On May 1, Sylvan Hart's flag-draped coffin was returned to Five Mile Bar and buried near the garden he had tended for over forty years. Rodney Cox performed the service. A black-powder, three-gun salute followed, but only one of the guns fired. It was one made by Hart.

On June 28, 1980, members of the Ee Da How Long Rifles, a black-powder club of which Hart was an honorary life member, made the trip up the Salmon River with the stone that now marks his resting place.

Visitors are still welcome at Five Mile Bar. They can examine Hart's cabins and view a video in which he shares examples of his artistry and tells of his life.

William Mackay

Mackay Bar is one of the better-known lodges and possesses the best landing strip on the Salmon River. William Mackay, however, was never able to call the place his own.

Born in New York in September 1846, he was the son of Irish immigrants. Like many young Irishmen, he made his way west for a better life, landing first in Montana before moving on to Idaho.

By 1899 Mackay had settled on the bar that now bears his name, at the mouth of the South Fork of the Salmon, on the south side of the river. He had a partner, W. S. Howenstine, and together they worked the area, building a cabin and other outbuildings. In the 1900 census, Mackay said he was the head of his household and owned his own home free and clear. He listed "gold miner" as his occupation.

He mined for the next nine years. In April 1905, he went into partnership with several prominent men from Warren, including Freeman Nethkin, William Kelly, and Fred Burgdorf. They staked the Mill Creek placer claim at the mouth of Mill Creek, two miles south of the confluence of the South Fork and the Main Salmon, at a site now known as the Badley Ranch. Four years later, Mackay and Howenstine staked a claim on Three Mile Creek, much closer to Mackay Bar. They called this twenty acres the Stuart placer claim.

In 1910 Mackay and Howenstine filed a homestead application on Mackay Bar. It was inspected by Forest Ranger Warren Cook, who verified that the men were using the bar for agriculture. In addition to their cabin, Mackay and Howenstine had built a hay shed, stable, a wood-storage shed, and two root cellars. In his field report, Cook reported all buildings were in good condition. But approval was delayed. Howenstine died, leaving Mackay the sole applicant. He worked the place, adding a hen house and a blacksmith shop. He also built a new cabin with eight-foot walls, a wooden floor, and a shake roof.

Only a pipe and pile of rocks mark the grave of William Mackay on the bench above Mackay Bar. It can be reached by following the road east from the south end of the Mackay Bar Bridge and then taking the trail south toward Mackay Creek. The bench lies on the east side of the trail.

Mackay died in December 1920 without obtaining title. Aware his homestead claim was transferable, Mackay left it and all his personal property to Perry Nethkin. In December 1922, Nethkin finally received title. Since then, the bar has changed hands many times.

The remains of Mackay's cabin can still be seen on the north side of Mackay Creek on the bluff above the Bar. His grave, with a spectacular view of the river, is located 100 yards west of the cabin.

Jim Rains

The Nez Perce War and the flight of Chief Joseph in 1877 are well documented in Idaho history. Two years later, on the banks of the South Fork of the Salmon River, a lesser known Indian uprising occurred. It left at least one grave in Warren.

James Rains came to Idaho County during the gold rush of the 1860s. Census records indicate he was born in Missouri, in the early 1830s, although other sources state he hailed from Oregon. He arrived with a brother, W. T. Rains, and together the two staked various claims in both the Warren and South Fork areas. James Rains also started several businesses, one of them a livery stable in Warren.

In 1872 Rains moved to the banks of the South Fork. He filed on a piece of ground on Mill Creek on the west side of the river, two miles south of the Main Salmon. He built a small cabin there and started a farm. Although he kept a house in Warren, he sold his other business interests there and called the South Fork home.

In April of 1874, Rains began another venture. The Idaho County commissioners gave him an exclusive license to build and maintain a bridge across the South Fork. As part of this agreement, he was to construct a trail from the east side of the bridge, running two miles north to the Main Salmon and then continuing twenty miles upstream on the Main Salmon. If he completed the project within one year, he would be allowed to charge travelers a toll. The county gave Rains the authority to charge one dollar for each horse and rider using the bridge. A person on foot would pay fifty cents.

Whether Rains completed the trail is not clear. A trail now runs from the end of a bridge by Rains' homestead down to Mackay Bar and a bit beyond. Perhaps some of it is his handiwork.

South Fork farming was prosperous for Rains. During this time he married Mary Webber, a Wisconsiner whose family had settled in Mount Idaho near Grangeville. While no marriage record survives, newspaper accounts and the census record report they were a couple. In 1878 their first son, Jesse, was born. In early August 1879, their second, John, followed.

In the fall of 1878 and spring of 1879, there was unrest among the Indians of central Idaho. On two different occasions, settlers in the area were ambushed and killed, reputedly by the Mountain Shoshoni, also known as Sheepeaters or Tukudika. One incident occurred on the South Fork at Elk Creek, where Hugh Johnson and Peter Dorsey were killed. In response, government troops were sent from Fort Howard, near Grangeville, to subdue the Indians. A detachment of sixty soldiers, led by Lieutenant Henry Catley, traveled to the South Fork by way of Florence, present-day Burgdorf, and Warren before arriving on the South Fork in early July. Catley proved a cowardly leader. His troops followed the Indians into the Big Creek drainage of the Middle Fork of the Salmon River and were involved in a skirmish, now known as the battle of Vinegar Hill. Catley retreated, crossed the South Fork, and marched to Burgdorf.

South Fork residents, Rains included, heard of Catley's retreat and as a precaution, packed up and moved to Warren. When no further word of trouble arrived, Rains left his family in Warren and returned to the South Fork to harvest his hay crop. James Edwards and Harry Serren accompanied him.

The three men went about their work. On August 15, they were joined by Albert Webber, Rains' brother-in-law. Haying was almost complete; they planned to finish up on the next day and return to Warren.

On the afternoon of August 16, Webber remained in the Rains' cabin to prepare dinner, while Edwards, Serren, and Rains went to the fields to finish their work. Although the men always carried their rifles into the fields, that afternoon they did not. As darkness approached, the three men came under fire. They fled into a creek bed and tried to make their way back to the house. Rains was then shot, once in the hip and once in the chest. Webber, in the house, returned fire, without effect. Serren and Edwards, realizing there was nothing else they could do, ran for help in Warren.

James Rains is buried in the Warren Cemetery, forty-five miles northeast of McCall, Idaho. The cemetery is located on top of a hill on the north side of Warren's main street.

Under cover of darkness, Rains crawled to the house. Webber, who had been shot in the shoulder, dragged him through the front door and laid him on a couch, where he died. By now the Indians had built fires around the house and Webber, realizing he had to escape or die, dug underneath the sill, crawled to an irrigation ditch, and made his way to Warren. Serren and Edwards were amazed by his arrival.

A party set out to protect the remaining homesteads on

the South Fork. Only the Rains Ranch had been attacked. The Indians burned the place and stole eight horses.

Early records report that Rains was buried at the ranch by the rescue party. Other accounts, however, state that his remains were collected and packed to Warren, where they were given a proper burial. Rains is on the sexton's list for the Warren cemetery, and a headboard, with an incorrect date, stands on his grave.

Mary Rains took her two young sons to Mount Idaho, where she lived with her father. Eventually, she married James Edwards and returned to Warren for a time. Jesse and John Rains grew to manhood, married, and lived out their days in Nez Perce County.

Richard Hambly

Richard Hambly was born in Pennsylvania in January of 1843, the son of English immigrants. At eighteen, he enlisted in the Union Army, where he was assigned to Company I of the 8th Pennsylvania Cavalry and fought at the Battle of Gettysburg. Some time after, he may have deserted. An article in the *Idaho Free Press* records that he had left the army without discharge papers. He also never filed for a veteran's pension.

He arrived in Idaho in the late 1860s, in the mining areas of Lemhi County. In 1870 he was in Leesburg, listing his occupation as placer miner. From there, he drifted west to Buffalo Hump and then south to the Warren area.

Hambly first established a camp on what is now known

as the Romine Ranch, one mile south of the Main Salmon up Warren Creek. He settled there in the early 1890s and staked the Hambly claim on April 10, 1891. In addition to his placer mining, he also tried cattle ranching, but ultimately he gave it up in order to concentrate on his mining.

He was an industrious man, staking at least twelve claims between 1896 and 1901. He also was part-owner of the well-known Klondyke claim. Of particular interest was the Secesh River area, where he staked several claims and spent much of his time. He and his partner, Ira McGary, also worked on Steamboat Summit, especially the Cape Nome claim. In 1897 Hambly reported it was yielding about seven dollars a day.

In 1900 Hambly was living in Warren, a tenant of Albert Blakely. He reported he was a mine laborer and had been steadily employed for the past year. Although he could be quick-tempered at times, he made a reputation for himself as a hard worker.

In 1906, near Warren, he struck an agreement with Steve Winchester, also of Warren. Together they decided to reopen the Rescue Mine, the one that established Warren. But Hambly filed the relocation papers without including Winchester's name. Hambly's inability to furnish military discharge papers, however, disallowed the filing. He abandoned the location, allowing his partner Ira McGary to file instead.

For two years, Winchester apparently stewed about not being included as a partner in the mine. He sued to get title to the claim himself and won. On April 18, 1908, McGary was served papers that required him to vacate the claim. Not wanting to lose it, he traveled to Grangeville to consult a lawyer, leaving Hambly to protect the site.

McGary and Hambly were to vacate the claim on April 21. Idaho County Deputy Sheriff Van de Venter was in Warren to make certain that the transfer to Winchester occurred peacefully. At 10:00 a.m., Hambly was waiting at the site. When the sheriff told him to leave, Hambly made it known he had no intention of giving up the claim without a fight. Then, Hambly fired his pistol four times at Winchester but missed. With his Iver-Johnson .38, Winchester shot Hambly three times. Hambly died an hour later.

By week's end, a frontier court was convened. Winchester was acquitted. Three witnesses to the shooting reported that Winchester acted in self-defense. Winchester then took sole possession of the Rescue Mine.

Hambly was buried in the Warren cemetery; however, the location of his grave has been lost. In 1913, Hambly's remaining property was auctioned, the balance of his estate went to Idaho County.

Frank Jordan

Warren Creek originates near Warren, Idaho, a mining town that in the 1860s boasted a population of over 6,000 miners. From Warren, the creek winds its way north for about sixteen miles down to its mouth at the Salmon River. Mining scars can be detected all along the creek. Frank Jordan lived and died on this stream.

Jordan was born in New York in 1842, to a father from Scotland and a mother from England. Jordan moved to the Midwest during the 1860s; then he was caught up in the fury of the Civil War and enlisted. His exact military experience is not known, but he stated in the 1910 census that he was a Civil War veteran.

Following the war, he moved farther west, arriving in Idaho sometime after 1900. He drifted into Idaho County and Warren, where he landed on Warren Creek, one mile south of the Salmon River. Here he built a cabin, put in a large garden, and did some placer mining.

Although Jordan chose an isolated spot, he was not without company. Since his cabin was located on the trail to Warren, he had frequent visitors. He also became good friends with Charles Shepp of the Shepp Ranch at the mouth of Crooked Creek on the Salmon River. Shepp must have taken a liking to him because he often mentioned Jordan in his diaries. He noted when Jordan came to dinner and when he showed up at the Bemis place to help Charlie and Polly Bemis put up their hay. Shepp, in turn, stopped at the Jordan Ranch and spent the night whenever he traveled the trail to Warren.

In March of 1906, Jordan staked a twenty-acre claim at the mouth of Warren Creek—the Idol—and over the next few years tried to make it productive. Most of his attention, however, was given to his garden. He raised ample vegetables for himself and many of the miners in Warren. He also grew tobacco and shared it with anyone who stayed at his place. Walter Mann, Payette National Forest district ranger, wrote that Jordan's tobacco was so strong that after one pipe full, he did not want another smoke for a week.

In 1910 Jordan began the paperwork for a homestead patent on his place. In December 1910, he filed for eighty acres. The following year, Walter Mann surveyed it. Jordan continued to live there, adding improvements and waiting for approval of his patent. He amended his application in 1918 and again in 1922.

Sometime after his last amendment, Jordan died. The only evidence is an entry in Charlie Shepp's diary on October 23, 1922, when Shepp visited Jordan's homestead; it took him four hours hiking to get there and when he arrived, two men were camped at Jordan's place, but Jordan himself was not there. No death record is on file with the county or state.

In July of 1929, a new homestead application for the Jordan place was filed by Roy Romine. His patent was granted in 1936.

Allegedly, Jordan is buried on the ranch, on a knoll, with a spring and trail near the grave.

Charlie Bemis

Charlie Bemis married well. Had it not been for his wife Polly, he would have been just another fortune seeker in Warren.

Bemis was born around 1850 to Alfred Bemis of Connecticut. The Bemis family was well established in that state, and Alfred may have acquired his wealth as a jeweler.

Alfred, accompanied by Charlie, arrived in the Warren area as early as 1863, where he set himself up as a miner and a banker. In Warren, the elder Bemis established Sanderson & Bemis, an enterprise that in addition to mining interests, also loaned money. When Alfred died in 1876, his death made the newspapers in Boise.

Charlie avoided the back-breaking work of placer mining. Seeing the value in the goldfields, and wanting nothing to do with stoop labor, Charlie, together with his father, frequently purchased claims and then leased them to miners. In 1870 he was astute enough to buy the rights to one of the arrastras located outside of Warren. With no stamp mills in the town, it was the next best device for extracting gold from the hard rock. Later, he added a second. In the 1880s, they were the only ore crushers working near Warren.

Bemis realized there was more money to be made in Warren by servicing the miners than from mining itself. To that end, he needed a tavern. On November 29, 1879, he traveled to Mount Idaho, where at a sheriff's auction, he bought his tavern and several other properties for $200. When he returned to Warren, he owned four prime properties on main street, including the Ripson Saloon. He would never mine again.

Since Bemis was an enterprising host, the tavern was successful. He brought in dancing girls for the miners, who paid both Bemis and the girls. He ran a first-rate establishment and earned a reputation as honest and upright. As a result, Bemis found himself in the banking business as well. Miners often came to Warren carrying their gold.

Fearing they would get drunk and lose it, they gave it to Bemis for safe keeping. He kept it secure in a safe, bought specifically for that purpose.

When Bemis met Polly, the Chinese slave girl who later became his wife, is unknown now. Polly arrived in Warren in 1872, the property of Hong King, who owned a dance hall next to Bemis' saloon. Bemis befriended her. When the miners at Hong King's became too rowdy, Polly ran across to Bemis' saloon to get help. Known to be adept with a gun, he never failed to assist her.

Legend has it that Bemis and Hong King were embroiled in a two-man poker game when Hong King staked Polly as his bet. When Bemis won the hand, he won Polly. This account is attributed to C. J. Czizek, Idaho's first mining inspector. Although Czizek retracted the story in 1933, it persists.

By the summer of 1880, Polly was working for Bemis in his saloon. He also helped Polly establish a boarding house, where Czizek lodged when in town, located next door to the saloon.

For the next ten years, the saloon business flourished, and Bemis became a leading citizen of Warren. He served as a deputy sheriff of the community and invested in property and mining claims around Warren and the South Fork. In the spring of 1887, he suffered a setback when his house burned to the ground. He lost about $2,500.

In September of 1890, Bemis finally met his match in a poker game. Two conflicting accounts exist. In one, Bemis won $150 from Johnny Cox in a poker game. Cox was angry and demanded his money back. When Bemis refused, Cox pulled his pistol and shot Bemis in the face. In the second version, Bemis lost $210 to Cox in a rigged poker game. He agreed to pay Cox the following morning, and when he offered $100 in a compromise, Cox refused and shot Bemis in the face.

Cox fled. The townspeople carried Bemis to his cabin and sent for Dr. Biddy in Grangeville. Biddy came but was pessimistic about the victim's prognosis because a bullet fragment remained lodged in his cheekbone. The doctor was convinced Bemis would die of blood poisoning shortly. Meanwhile, the men of Warren raised $300 and sent Harry Cone to capture Cox and bring him to justice. He found him in Pocatello playing poker. He took Cox to Lewiston, where he was charged with assault with a deadly weapon. In October of 1891, Cox was sentenced to five years. He served two.

Under the watchful eye of Polly, Bemis gradually recovered and eventually went back to work at his saloon. With gratitude to Polly, and perhaps because of new deportation laws, on August 13, 1894, he and Polly were married by the justice of the peace in Warren.

Not long afterward, they moved down to the Salmon River across the river from Crooked Creek, where they built a cabin and began a garden. Since Bemis leased his properties in Warren, the couple had an income to supplement what they could grow on the river. In March 1899, Bemis filed a mining claim on the site, ensuring their rights. He filed on twenty-seven acres with 1,200 feet of river frontage.

Life was pleasant on the river. They became friends with Charlie Shepp and Peter Klinkhammer, who lived on the opposite shore. Bemis ferried people across the river with a small rowboat and did not charge for his services. They opened their home to travelers and were known as gracious hosts.

While some report Bemis was an invalid during this time, he remained fairly active. He left most chores, however, to Polly. He hunted and fished and spent time target shooting with Shepp. He supervised as Shepp and Frank Jordan from up the river plowed the garden and cut the hay on the bar. He also made frequent trips to Warren to check on his properties. In September of 1904, he lost them when a fire swept through Warren, destroying all of his buildings as well as those of others. Each summer thereafter, he and Polly rode to Warren to sell their produce, and Bemis supplemented their income by playing poker.

Eventually, however, Bemis' health deteriorated. By 1919 he was bedridden and relied on Shepp and Klinkhammer to help Polly with the place. In order that he could check on them regularly, Shepp ran a battery phone line from his house to the Bemis' cabin.

On the night of August 16, 1922, the Bemis cabin caught fire. According to Shepp: "Bemis house burned at midnight... Got the old man out by the skin of my teeth." The house was destroyed, including its contents. Shepp managed to get Polly and Bemis over to his place. The next day he built a bed for Bemis, and the couple stayed there until Bemis died on the morning of October 29.

Charlie Bemis was the first known burial at the Shepp Ranch.

Shepp recruited two miners from the War Eagle Mine to help bury Bemis. As Polly requested, he was buried according to Chinese custom on a south-facing slope overlooking the river.

Polly lived for eleven more years and has become an Idaho icon. Bemis is remembered because he was her husband.

Charles Shepp

Only Merriwether Lewis left as much of himself to history as Charlie Shepp. From 1902 until his death in 1937, Shepp chronicled his life on the Salmon River in detail. From his writings it is clear that Shepp had a great appreciation for hard work, his friends, and the world around him.

Shepp was born in Iowa in 1861. He had several brothers and sisters, but was particularly close to his sister Nellie, who went by the family's original name, Shupp. He regularly corresponded with her from his ranch on the Salmon River.

By 1880 Charlie had begun his journey west. He was in Wyoming for a time, where he worked as a carpenter before moving on to Seattle. From Seattle, he went by passenger ship to Alaska to join the Klondike gold rush there. He must have found the stories of gold bigger than life, for by 1899, he was back in the states, in the Buffalo Hump area of Idaho County. He staked his first claim, the Hyak, in the Robbins District the same year.

Shepp's relationship with Charlie and Polly Bemis, who lived across the Salmon River from Crooked Creek, began soon after his arrival in Idaho. For the next thirty-four years, they were best friends. There is scarcely an entry in his diary that does not mention the couple. He also picked up a younger partner, Pete Klinkhammer, whose work habits and character complemented his own. The two remained partners until Shepp's death.

As soon as he arrived in the area, Shepp took a liking to the Crooked Creek drainage, where the creek met the Salmon River, thirty-seven miles upstream from Riggins. Originally settled by Pete Mallick, the place subsequently was occupied by Charlie Williams and "Four-eyed" Smith. In 1909 Shepp and Klinkhammer bought the ranch from Smith for $1,000.

Shepp's diaries are filled with the details of his life, working the mines in the spring and fall, cutting wood in the winter, tending to his garden in the summer. He had regular visitors, mentioned in his diary by first or last name, never both. He also recorded his trips to the Bemis' place and spent most of his holidays there. His finances were recorded meticulously. He knew how much he owed, to whom, and how much he was owed. He kept a close watch on the weather. On July 28, 1905, he recorded that a hailstorm "cut up the garden bed." March 11, 1906, was the coldest day Shepp had ever seen, "Everything in the house froze."

Many entries ended the same way: "It was a fine day." In spite of the hard work, Shepp clearly loved his life. He took a particular interest in his animals. His dogs are mentioned by name, as are his horses. When his horses were lost, he recorded it; then he recorded where and when they were found. Every lamb and calf born on the ranch was duly noted. A hunter, he chronicled his successes and his failures. He did not boast about his shooting prowess. He and Bemis often took target practice together and turned it into a friendly contest. Bemis usually won.

In 1909, with the ranch in their possession, Shepp and Klinkhammer began numerous improvements. Their plan was to supplement their income with a garden and orchard that would provide food for the miners in Buffalo Hump, Warren, and Dixie. They built a new cabin of whipsawed lumber with tongue-and-groove flooring and a shake roof. They added a blacksmith's shop, a chicken coop, and a root cellar. After all the improvements, Charlie Shepp filed for a homestead patent on 135 acres, and it was granted in September 1922. On June 28, 1923, it was recorded. The same day, Shepp sold one-half interest to Peter Klinkhammer for $2,500.

Their efforts paid off. While Klinkhammer packed the produce to the mining camps, Shepp tended the garden. The Shepp Ranch was known for its apples; every fall, they packed several hundred pounds of them to the miners. They also grew cherries, apricots, and varieties of other fruit. Vegetables such as corn, squash, turnips, carrots, and potatoes, stored in the root cellar, were plentiful. Shepp also grew tobacco and hops. In addition to his own chores, he helped at the Bemis' place across the river.

Aside from his garden, Shepp's chief interest was radios. He built his own sets and early pictures of his house show a radio antenna perched on the roof. His diaries log the stations he received. Once the phone line from his house to the Bemis' cabin was strung, he called Polly—sometimes three times a day—to check on her.

Shepp also was aging. A diary entry in July 1933 acknowledges the long life he has already lived. "Went to see Polly. Polly's birthday Sept. 11. She will be 80. My birthday, 73."

It is clear from diary entries that year that Shepp was slowing down, especially after Polly's death in November. In December, Alex Blain moved in with him. Although Shepp never stated it directly, Blain must have been employed by him because Shepp kept track of all the jobs he assigned to Blain. His journal entries became shorter—some only three or four words.

In 1935 Shepp left the ranch for several months. At first Blain was caretaker, but then Shepp rented the place, and Blain moved across the river to the Bemis' place. Klinkhammer's whereabouts at this time are not known. When Shepp returned, Blain continued to stay at the Bemis' place, but once again became Shepp's hired hand. On November 25, 1935, Shepp sold his half of the ranch to Klinkhammer for one dollar.

In the spring of 1936, Shepp replanted his garden. He continued to write in his diary, but some days there is no more than a checkmark. For the first time he simply wrote the word "rest" as his day's activity. By the summer and fall, he seemed to be feeling better. He traveled to Grangeville for Border Days, took his annual winter order for Montgomery Ward to Dixie, and hauled 500 pounds of apples to Warren. And he made a rigorous November trip, seventeen miles to Dixie, to vote in the general election.

By 1937 Shepp's handwriting was almost illegible. Still he continued to record the weather (-20 degrees in late January) and made plans for his garden. From May until September of 1937, however, there are no diary entries and no explanation. In a September entry he simply says that he had been sick, but is feeling better. By early October, he was sawing wood, picking apples, and making daily trips across the river to visit Blain.

Charlie Shepp is buried just northeast of the main lodge at the Shepp Ranch.

On October 8, 1937, Shepp wrote in his diary that he was sick. Bill Morris spent the night with him, and then headed to Dixie the next day. Morris returned on October 11 and stayed at the ranch. Shepp noted that he, himself, was "very ill."

For the rest of the month, the entries only concern Shepp's health and the weather: "a little better," "so, so," or "the same." Morris stayed on. On October 31, Shepp was again well enough to visit Blain.

In November Shepp was bedridden. Many visitors are

noted in his diary, including Captain Guleke. Klinkhammer also arrived. On November 20, Shepp wrote that Morris traveled to T-bone Creek downriver and returned that evening. It was the last entry. Although he had written out the dates for the rest of the month, nothing was recorded.

The date of Shepp's death is unknown; there is even some question as to the year. Sister Alfreda Elsensohn, in *Pioneer Days in Idaho County*, says Shepp died in 1936. Her source was Klinkhammer. Paul Filer, who bought the Shepp Ranch from Klinkhammer, made the grave marker for Shepp based on that information. No official death record for Shepp exists, but the diary ends in 1937. The inconsistency, for now, cannot be resolved.

Shepp was buried near the house that he helped build. Klinkhammer kept the homestead until he sold it to Paul Filer in 1950. It remains a privately-owned resort.

Alex Blain

In the late 1920s, Alex Blain was a character in Dixie, Idaho. Whenever he passed through, the Dixie reporter for the *Idaho County Free Press* took notice.

Other than that he was born in 1859, little is known about him. He does not appear in any Idaho census and, at least in Idaho County, staked no mining claims. According to Paul Filer, former owner of the Shepp Ranch, Blain was a large man of Scottish descent. His name also appears as "Blaine" in some accounts.

He was a handyman, traveling from place to place doing odd jobs. Though in the late 1920s he called Dixie home, he also spent time in Elk City, on Middle Fork tributary Big Creek, and along the Salmon River. No matter where he was, he was always busy.

In January of 1929, Blain left Dixie and traveled seventeen miles south to the Shepp Ranch, and as mentioned earlier, went to work for Charlie Shepp. The relationship with Shepp and the ranch continued until Blain's death.

In addition to his Shepp Ranch stints, Blain worked in different mines in the Buffalo Hump area, including the War Eagle. He also worked for the Forest Service from time to time, mostly as a trail builder. He constructed much of the trail along the north side of the Salmon River between the Shepp Ranch and Sheep Creek.

In 1932, tired of working for others, Blain bought the Dixie Hotel. He promptly closed it, planning major renovations. Perhaps he ran out of money or his plans were too grandiose, because one month later, he sold the place. As a hired hand, he returned to jobs such as re-roofing houses in Elk City and clearing property for a landowner on Big Creek .

In 1933 Blain lived at the Shepp Ranch. He remained in this area for the next seven years, either staying with Shepp or living at the Bemis' place across the river. Even in his seventies, Blain worked as hard as any younger man.

According to Shepp's diaries, in December 1933, Blain was mending fence, fixing the cellar door, and bringing in firewood. In spring 1934, he was in charge of rounding up the horses, burning the trash, and plowing the garden.

Of the graves at the Shepp Ranch, Alex Blain's is closest to the river. Permission to visit it should be requested first.

Whenever Shepp left the ranch, he left in charge.

In 1935 Shepp's health dictated he leave the ranch for a few months. Blain cared for it until Shepp decided to rent it. Then Blain moved across the river into Polly Bemis' cabin and remained there until Shepp's death in 1937. When Shepp died, Blain moved back into the Shepp Ranch house. In his late seventies, he stayed there maintaining it.

The exact circumstances of Blain's death are unknown, but one can surmise that he succumbed to the infirmities of age.

When he died in 1940, no one summoned the sheriff or coroner, and no death notice appeared in the Grangeville paper. He was buried near the main house at the Shepp Ranch next to his old friend, Charlie Shepp. Paul Filer made the bronze plaque marking his grave.

J. W. Jones

Not well known in life, it is scarcely remarkable that J. W. Jones' grave is unmarked in death.

Jones was an eccentric loner who arrived on the Salmon River during the summer of 1927. He lived along the banks of Crooked Creek, upstream from the Shepp Ranch, and did his best to avoid strangers. He was so reclusive that no one even knew his first name.

He lived meagerly, surviving on the fish he caught in the creek and the berries he gathered along its banks. He preferred a small, insubstantial camp hidden in the underbrush near the Shepp Ranch. He always carried his belongings in a small pack. When people approached, he refused to talk. He also refused any offer of supplies or assistance from nearby river residents. He did do some prospecting along Crooked Creek, but the results were not a source of income.

On August 10, 1927, Forest Service employees working in the area found him dead near his camp. On searching his shelter, they found his diary, since lost. The last entry was dated August 5, 1927.

The Forest Service employees called the sheriff in Grangeville, who advised them to bury Jones on Crooked Creek, and they did. Jones' grave is just another now lost on the River of No Return.

Polly Bemis

Polly Bemis, the diminutive Chinese woman who won the hearts of miners and travelers up and down the Salmon River, is a special figure in Idaho history.

Bemis was born in northern China on September 11, 1853. Her feet were bound when she was a little girl, a custom in upper-class Chinese families, indicating her family was prosperous. However, when Bemis was in her teens, her family fell on hard times. In order to save the rest of the family, her father traded her for money to buy seeds.

Bemis was smuggled into the United States, first landing in San Francisco. She was then taken to Portland. She was sold there for $2,500 to a man named Hong King, who transported her to Warren, Idaho, where she worked in his dance hall and took care of him. She was nineteen years old, five feet tall, trim, with jet black hair pulled back in a bun.

Tradition says she was given the name "Polly" on the day of her arrival in Warren, when a young miner helped her from her horse and said, "Here's Polly." She said her Chinese name was Lalu Nathoy—the name recorded on her residency papers. On her marriage license, her name is listed as "Polly Hathey."

Polly was the only Chinese woman in Warren. During this time she met Charlie Bemis, who, as mentioned earlier, owned a saloon next door to Hong King's dance hall.

How Polly gained her release from Hong King is now uncertain. The story most often repeated is that Hong King offered her as security in a poker game, and Charlie won the hand. Peter Klinkhammer, Polly's friend after she moved to the river, believed Charlie purchased Polly to save her from working for Hong King.

By the 1880 census, Polly was living in the same household as Charlie Bemis and was listed as a widow. According to Dr. Priscilla Wegars, who has done extensive historical research on Polly and the Chinese in Idaho, she would have

Polly Bemis' grave lies just south of her restored cabin on the Salmon River, across from the Shepp Ranch. A path from the river leads to the site.

used the widow designation if her master had died. It is possible, therefore, that she was independent because Hong King was dead. Furthermore, Hong King is not listed in the 1880 Idaho census.

Polly moved into a two-story house next to that of Charlie Bemis. For the next ten years, she ran a boarding house, did laundry, and kept house for Charlie. It was during this time that Polly endeared herself to the people of Warren. Incredibly industrious, she not only ran a spotless boarding house but learned to cook and excelled at it. For the miners, she kept their clothes cleaned and patched, washing on Tuesdays and ironing on Wednesdays. She still worked in Charlie's saloon as a hostess and often accompanied him to town dances and other civic functions.

In September 1890, when Charlie's gambling nearly cost him his life, Polly refused to accept the doctor's prognosis and over the course of several weeks, she nursed him back to health. Using a crochet hook and a razor, she removed the bone and bullet fragments, then used an herbal concoction to heal his wound.

In 1894 Polly was threatened with deportation. According to the rules established by the Chinese Exclusion Acts of 1892-1893, all Chinese immigrants were required to register with the federal government. Polly, along with about 150 other Chinese living in Idaho County, were to meet with a representative of the Internal Revenue Service in Grangeville, but the representative never appeared. Charlie Bemis resolved the predicament by marrying Polly on August 13, 1894, in Warren. Two years later, Polly was granted a certificate of residency by the U. S. District Court.

The couple left Warren and traveled north to the Salmon River, where they established the Bemis Ranch. They built a cabin, planted fruit trees, and put in a sizable garden. Polly became adept at fishing, and her garden was one of the more productive on the river. For the next twenty-seven years, Polly and Charlie would live comfortably on the Salmon River. As Charlie's health began to fail, she became the principle provider.

By 1919 Charlie was an invalid. Shepp and Klinkhammer helped Polly with the arduous chores. Shepp also saved her life on the night of August 16, 1922, when the Bemis' cabin caught fire.

After Bemis died, Polly returned to Warren, where she lived for two years. On two occasions she left to experience life outside the mining camp. In August 1923, she visited Grangeville, where she was treated as a celebrity, viewing her first movie and riding on a train for the first time. In 1924 she visited Boise and she saw her first streetcar and took a ride in an elevator.

Shepp kept in touch with her, and in the fall of 1923, he visited her in Warren. When he returned to the river, he and Klinkhammer built a new cabin for her; the following summer, Klinkhammer went to Warren and brought Polly back to the river. She agreed that if they would look after her, she would leave them her place. In 1929 Klinkhammer filed for a homestead on the Bemis Ranch. It included the log cabin, a log blacksmith's shop, and a log hayshed, on twenty-seven acres. The patent was granted in 1936.

Polly spent her final years on the river. Shepp checked on her often. The men did all of the heavy work and brought supplies from Dixie, seventeen miles by trail, when she needed them.

In the summer of 1933, Polly's health began to fail. On Friday, August 4, Shepp rowed across the river and found her lying on the ground outside her house. In his diary, Shepp noted that she was "nearly helpless."

The next day, he called Frank McGrane in Grangeville and informed him of her condition. That afternoon, Klinkhammer and a man named Anderson arrived at the Shepp Ranch. The next morning, they put Polly on a horse and packed her to the Halfway House near Dixie. She was taken by ambulance to Grangeville, where she was placed in a nursing home. McGrane called Shepp on August 11 and told him Polly was doing "okay." For the rest of the summer and into the fall, Shepp and Klinkhammer took care of her place, harvested her vegetables, picked her fruit. On October 25, Shepp went across the river and turned off the irrigation water.

On September 11, 1933, Polly turned eighty in the nursing home. She became so ill she was taken to the county hospital. When visitors tried to be optimistic about her recovery, she smiled and said, "Me too old to get well."

She died on the afternoon of November 6, 1933. Shepp was informed by telephone. He noted: "Polly passed away this afternoon," and underlined it.

Funeral services for Polly were held on November 8 at 10:00 a.m. Neither Shepp nor Klinkhammer could attend because winter weather had already set in. Despite her request to be buried on the river, she was laid to rest in the Prairie View Cemetery in Grangeville.

The Bemis' property changed hands several times over the years. In 1987 Jim Campbell, co-owner of the Bemis' homestead, restored Polly's cabin and then had her remains flown to the site and reinterred. In 1989 Polly's cabin was added to the National Register of Historic Places. Her grave lies a few feet from her cabin, within sight of the Salmon River.

James Hemstock

Fewer than seventy-five feet from the Salmon River, just above the high water mark, is the grave of James Hemstock. So inconspicuous is it that most people pass by without noticing.

Hemstock was born in 1841, in Illinois, the second son of Thomas and Martha Hemstock. Thomas Hemstock, a farmer, raised a family of four boys: George, James, John, and Harlan.

George and James struck out together. In 1870 they were living in Union, Storey County, Iowa, where both were employed as carpenters. The 1870 Iowa census lists James' possessions as worth $400.

By the 1890s, Hemstock was in Idaho, working the tail end of the gold rush in Florence. He also did some trapping on the side. Hemstock was well known around Florence and in the nearby Buffalo Hump District.

James Hemstock is buried on the trail on the north side of the Salmon River, approximately three-quarters of a mile upstream from Sheep Creek. The grave is located on the river side of the trail.

How he provided for himself is not clear—his name is largely absent from mining records kept at the time. He did, however, stake a claim on January 1, 1908, in the Marshall Mining District. He and six other persons claimed the 140-acre Buckeye placer claim on Fall Creek, a tributary of the Main Salmon.

The Buckeye claim was worthless, because within a year, Hemstock was in a cabin on Elk Creek, on the north side of the Salmon River. He went to the cabin intending to spend the winter trapping and placer mining.

In February, 1909, word reached the mining camps and the Shepp Ranch on Crooked Creek that Hemstock was ill with dropsy. Pete Klinkhammer sought out two miners, Jack

Conroy and Ed Bronton, and asked them to go with him to Hemstock's cabin. They reached it on February 27, planning to take him to Mount Idaho, where there was a doctor. One report states that the men used a travois behind a mule to haul Hemstock from his cabin to a pack trail along the river, where he died. According to Klinkhammer, however, they managed to get Hemstock onto a horse, but two miles later, he was in such pain that he asked to get off. At that point, he died. Hemstock was an ample man, and the three rescuers decided it was best to bury him on the spot. Klinkhammer related the story to Charlie Shepp, who recorded in his diary that Pete "had a devil of a time" with Hemstock. Klinkhammer later recalled that the trapper's death "was the nicest thing he could have done for us."

Hemstock's grave is marked with a weathered, black granite stone carved in January 1958 by Glen Rice, a once Salmon River guide and packer employed at Shepp Ranch.

Clarence Rowley

For Clarence Rowley, the opportunity to earn a living in the mountains of Idaho held more appeal than laboring as a farmhand on the Palouse.

Rowley was born on November 2, 1879, in Dayton, Washington, the son of Robert and Nettie Rowley. Robert, a Wisconsin native, supported his family by working in a sawmill. Nettie, from Oregon, stayed at home with their children. In addition to Clarence, they had Flora, born in 1876,

The grave of Clarence Rowley lies 200 yards upriver from the north end of the Wind River Pack Bridge, twenty-three miles east of Riggins.

and Harry, born in 1890.

By the mid-1890s, Clarence had left his parents and was living in Latah County near Moscow. In September of 1896, he and a partner, T. S. Edmunson, paid $525 for the Avalanche mining claim in the Dixie Mining District in Idaho County.

The winter of 1898 was one of the hardest weathered by residents of Warren and Florence. Temperatures in February and March dipped to 25 below zero, and on March 26, Florence still had five feet of snow—an inopportune time for Rowley to visit his claims in the Marshall Mining District south of Florence.

Sometime in late February 1898, the inexperienced Rowley headed to the Kimberly Mine, located in the mountains south of Wind River, well above the Salmon River. He was caught in a snow storm and froze to death alone on the trail. The miners who found him packed his body to the mouth of Wind River and buried him there.

Rowley's grave was marked with a wooden headboard. By the 1960s, the board was gone. Ace Barton and Mrs. Joe Crozier from Riggins made the present marker, using concrete hauled from the Wind River bridge abutments.

Family records indicate Rowley died in 1902, but do not give a cause. With no public death record available, the discrepancy is now irreconcilable.

Charles White

Pouring out of Buffalo Hump country, Wind River flows nine miles, falling nearly 5,000 feet before it empties into the Salmon River twenty-one miles east of Riggins.

On January 3, 1919, a rancher and miner from Grangeville, J. C. White, also known as Charles White, located the Wind River claim. White worked it for several months, but on April 7, 1919, he sold it to another rancher and miner, Neil McMeekin, who already had a place two miles up Wind River. McMeekin paid $100 for the claim, which included twenty acres and a three-room cabin located near the mouth of Wind

River. McMeekin was ready to take possession in early April, but White apparently changed his mind.

Even though he had sold the claim, White continued to live in the cabin, sharing the space with McMeekin. At first the men got along, but tensions flared as White prepared to move. He insisted that some of the items in the cabin were his personal property, not part of the sale, and said he planned to take them with him when he left.

McMeekin was agreeable, letting White take some tools and supplies in order to avoid a confrontation. His patience ran out, however, when White decided he wanted four earthen crocks in which McMeekin had stored staples. Initially, McMeekin refused to relinquish any of them, saying White had no use for them. White persisted, so McMeekin compromised, surrendering two. The day before he was to leave, White took the two crocks and put them in a cellar where he kept his other personal belongings. At the same time, McMeekin gathered some staples for White, including sugar, which he put in a gunny sack.

On the morning of May 5, McMeekin found that White had removed a third crock, but made no mention of it until White went after the fourth crock for the sugar. McMeekin refused and a fight ensued. According to McMeekin, White hit him; he retaliated by shoving White toward the door. White allegedly reached outside the door and grabbed a shovel. At the same time, McMeekin snatched a .38 caliber Colt out of a drawer. As the two men clashed, McMeekin fired three times. He hit White in the chest, in the right shoulder, and in the back of the head. (White's hat, with a

Charles White is buried on the bar at Wind River, once his home.

bullet hole in the back, was presented as evidence at McMeekin's trial.)

After the shooting, McMeekin walked up the Wind River trail to find his brother. Sam McMeekin and Bob Hiland returned with him to the cabin and found White dead. At that point, Neil McMeekin, aware that he had to meet with the authorities, went to the Parisot Mine to give himself up. Emile Parisot advised McMeekin to go to the Scott Ranch, west of the Parisot Mine, and turn himself in to H. R. Hinkson, the area constable, which he did. Hinkson took him to Grangeville, where he was charged with first degree murder. Meanwhile, Idaho County Sheriff W. H. Eller traveled to the murder site.

The first men on the scene, Sam McMeekin, Bob Hiland, Emile Parisot, and Ray Parisot, found White lying on his back in the doorway of the cabin. They checked his wounds, then waited for the sheriff. As the sun heated up the canyon, the men moved White under a tree on the west bank of Wind River and covered him with a tent. The sheriff found him there.

Realizing it was too warm and too far to transport the body to Grangeville, he completed his investigation on site. The Parisots brought lumber from their mine, planed it, and nailed a coffin together. At the sheriff's direction, White was buried on the bar where Wind River flows into the Salmon.

Neil McMeekin's trial lasted two days. He argued that he killed White in self-defense. The jury, after deliberating for four hours on September 17, 1919, found him not guilty.

White's gravesite is easily visible from the Wind River trail, marked by a concrete cross also installed by Ace Barton and Mrs. Joe Crozier when they marked the Rowley grave.

Emile Parisot

The lonely grave of E. A. Parisot is situated high on a promontory overlooking the Salmon River Breaks.

Parisot was born in Keweenaw County, Michigan, the son

of French immigrants. His parents, Theophilus Parisot and Marianne Voiland Parisot, arrived in the United States in the 1850s. Theophilus worked as a farmhand to support his family, which by the mid-1860s included Mary, John, Emile, and Albert. Emile was born in 1862, third of the four children.

Early life was difficult for Emile; his parents divorced in 1874. In the 1880s, Emile and his brother John traveled west to Montana. There Emile met and married Mary Nave. They resided in Lewiston, Montana, long enough to have a son, Raymond. But by 1893, Parisot had left his wife and son in favor of Idaho.

Parisot drifted into Grangeville, where he joined some other men in mining interests on the South Fork of the Clearwater River. In March of 1893, he staked three claims on the Clearwater: the Golden Era, the Enterprise, and the Industry. In April of 1895, he also staked the Badger claim in the same area. Shortly afterwards, he left the Clearwater drainage for Florence and the Salmon River.

In November 1895, Parisot began buying quartz claims in Florence, including the Eagle Bird Mine, for $350 dollars. Over the next ten years, he purchased numerous hard-rock and placer claims in Florence and Buffalo Hump. Among them were the Cumberland claim, the Atlas Mine, and the Colonel Sellers claim, for which he paid $1,000.

Besides his mining ventures, Parisot was involved in the publishing business. In the late 1890s, Florence was still a settlement that warranted a weekly newspaper, and along with a partner, D. C. Boyd, every Saturday he printed the *Florence Miner*. Residents paid nine dollars for a six-month subscription.

Parisot's mining investments required frequent trips to Grangeville, where he was known for his mining and publishing. During these trips he visited with May Vinson, whose family was well established. On May 5, 1903, the two were married.

Their son, Clement King, was born on January 24, 1904. By 1907, however, Emile and May had gone their separate ways. May moved with her son to Washington state, while Parisot returned to his mines in Florence. But he did not forget

The three mile trail to the Bullion Mine, where Emile Parisot is buried, takes off from the north end of the Wind River Pack Bridge. From the mine entrance, the grave is located to the south on a promontory overlooking the Salmon River canyon.

his son. In October of 1909, he struck a new claim in the Florence Mining District and called it the "Clement King."

In 1910, when Parisot was living in a Grangeville boarding house, his census form reveals he had not yet divorced May. He simply stated that he was a gold miner, working on his own.

In October of 1915, Parisot acquired the Bullion Mine. Originally staked by a man named Bennett in 1906, the mine was forfeited to Idaho County for unpaid taxes. Parisot purchased it from the county for $23.50. In addition, Parisot also staked two new mines the following year, the Atlantic and the Pacific.

In May of 1916, he began selling shares in the Bullion. Over the next three years he sold his holdings in installments, all to John Cooke from Spokane, Washington. By October 1919, Parisot had parted with his entire interest in the mine for "one dollar and other valuable considerations."

He continued to manage the Bullion, but in January of 1920, he contracted pneumonia. Although treated by Dr. Foskett from Whitebird, Parisot failed to improve. Aware of his approaching death, he rode to Grangeville, where he settled his business affairs, then returned to the mine and gave burial instructions to his son Raymond, who had earlier joined his father's mining operation.

Parisot died on March 17, 1920. At his request, he was buried on a point overlooking the Salmon River Canyon, less than one-quarter mile from the mouth of the Bullion Mine. In 1974 the ashes of Raymond, who left the Salmon River shortly after his father died, were also buried there.

Joseph Rogers

Near the end of the Salmon River Road, twenty-four miles east of Riggins, lies a solitary grave on the south side of the road. It may contain the remains of Joe Rogers.

Rogers was a miner working out of the Spokane area in the late 1800s, having come west from Vermont, where he was born in 1856. He worked in the mines of Shoshone County, Idaho for a short time before turning his attention to placer mining in the Salmon River country.

Rogers filed his first claim in Idaho County in May of 1900, when he paid $250 for the Wild Buffalo in the Robbins District. Over the next two years, he picked up several more claims on the Salmon, then focused on the Rapid River area. In 1902 he was living in Pollack, Idaho, and worked a location on Rapid River called the Lake View claim.

At this time, Rogers became friends with several men living at Goff on Race Creek, just north of present-day Riggins. Rogers formed a partnership with them, including J. O. Levander, who ran the hotel and way station at Goff. In the summer of 1909, Rogers and Levander became partners in a larger mining venture on the Main Salmon: the Yellow Boy, Sunshine, Edith, and Monte Christo claims. Located on the north bank of the Salmon, they were upriver from Riggins and stretched seven miles from Berg Creek to Kelly Creek.

In January of 1910, Rogers' body was found on the trail to the Marshall mines near Florence, where he still had several claims. According to accounts in the *Idaho County Free Press*, Rogers was caught in a snowstorm and froze to death on the trail. Old timers, however, said that Rogers accidentally shot himself in the leg and, unable to get help, died by the river.

Mystery also surrounds Rogers' gravesite. The *Free Press* noted that Rogers' friends from Goff planned to retrieve his body and take it back to Goff for burial. Although sexton's records in the Riggins cemetery include a Joe Rogers, no marker for the grave exists. Possibly, his friends buried him where they found him, and cemetery records simply noted his death.

This speculation is supported by the recollection of Lum Turner, who lived on the river road near the gravesite for over forty years. Turner, a Civilian Conservation Corps foreman, moved the grave in the 1930s, when CCC workers were building the Salmon River Road, because the original grave was in the path of the new road. According to him, he reburied the body above the road cut.

Presently, the grave is marked with a cairn shadowed by a Douglas fir blazed with a cross.

William Soards

Although the Salmon River offered a plentiful life to some along its banks, for others it brought only tragedy.

What is known about William Soards is sketchy. Census records contain inconsistencies; most of the evidence, however, confirms he was born in Missouri in the 1850s. He remained there long enough to marry Emma Newton in Jackson, Missouri, in August 1879. Emma died before William left for Idaho. He never remarried.

Soards arrived in Idaho with his brother Henry Soards prior to 1900. They settled in Nez Perce County, where both of them became sheep ranchers. They found easy enemies among the cattle ranchers on the Camas Prairie, and Henry's behavior, in particular, did not endear him to anyone. His quick temper and truculent disposition led to many barroom brawls in Grangeville.

The brothers eventually moved closer to the Salmon River, Henry just downriver from Whitebird; William established a ranch near present-day Winchester, east of Lewiston. He remained there until 1920. Henry, angering the wrong person, was murdered on his place in 1918. No one was charged.

In 1919 Henry's sons, Royston and Albert, established a homestead at the mouth of French Creek on the Salmon River. Their mother, Mattie Soards, moved in with them. William eventually joined them there, settling into a cabin across the river from French Creek at Knott's Ferry.

In August of 1921, Mattie went searching for several head of their cattle on the bluffs overlooking the Salmon. She followed the trail up the side of the canyon, then attempted a short cut, but slipped and fell to her death. Her body was found at the river's edge.

Before his mother's death, Royston moved to Riggins. Albert remained on the river, working the homestead and looking after his uncle. William's health declined, and in early 1922, he suffered two strokes, which left him partially paralyzed and unable to work. Fearful another stroke might leave him helpless, in late September of that year, he swallowed strychnine.

Albert Soards was in Grangeville loading freight at the time of his uncle's suicide. When he returned, he went to check on his uncle and found his decomposed body lying on the bed in his cabin.

Albert sent word to the Idaho County coroner, A. J. Maugg, who held an inquest at the site. He determined suicide was the cause of death and ordered the body buried there. The men wrapped it in canvas, placed it in a wooden box, and buried it near the cabin.

No stone or headboard marks the grave today. Local oral tradition situates it next to the trail, one-half mile east of the Standish homestead.

Swanson Knudson

Sven Knudson, Swan Knootsen, Swanson Knudson. Few liked him and no one knew how to spell his name.

Knudson arrived on the Salmon River in 1895. Originally from Spokane, he moved to Idaho County to work on the Elk City and Salmon River wagon roads. When the work was completed, Knudson stayed on at French Creek, where he was befriended by Charley Waldon. Waldon had settled a place on the east side of French Creek, about one mile up from the Salmon River. When Waldon could no longer take care of his place because of his age, he gave it to Knudson.

Knudson was not a miner; he earned his living by growing vegetables and raising cattle, which he sold to miners. He often loaded his pack horses with fresh meat and rode to Warren, or crossed the river and took the trail past the Scott Ranch to Florence.

It may have been on one of these trips to Florence that he met his wife. On January 25, 1899, Knudson married Anna Scott, widow of Newton Scott. Newton had died in November 1897 after being struck by a falling tree on the trail between Florence and Slate Creek.

Anna must have been unaware of Knudson's disposition, but people on the river were convinced she had married the devil. Most of his neighbors agreed he was honest and industrious, yet they avoided him because they considered him "quarrelsome." He was known to pick fights and reportedly whipped at least two of his neighbors. He had many enemies.

In the fall of 1900, someone took a shot at Knudson as he rode along the trail to Florence. His horse was killed, but Knudson survived.

On August 17, 1901, Knudson loaded two pack horses with beef and headed toward Florence. The next day, two miners found his body on the trail. He had been shot three times, including once in each arm. One of his horses also had been shot. When officials investigated, they found evidence that the shooter had been waiting in ambush. No other clues were found, and the murder was never solved. Knudson was buried near the trail where his body was found. His grave was never marked.

Eight months later, on April 7, 1902, Anna Knudson gave birth to Knudson's only child, a daughter.

Christopher Arnold

Christopher Arnold came to America as a fortune seeker. His travels took him to the goldfields of Idaho County.

Arnold was born in Greiz, Germany in June 1849. When he was twenty-one, he left his home from the Port of Bremen aboard the *S.S. Hansa* and sailed to America, arriving in New York on March 3, 1871. His ship papers reveal he traveled alone and had no formal occupation.

When he arrived in Idaho is unclear. Mining records do not show any claims from Arnold before 1890. He also does not appear in any Idaho census until 1900. By that time he had become a naturalized citizen.

Arnold's first recorded mining efforts were in the Florence District, where he staked claims on the Humboldt and Genesee mines in the summer of 1895. In 1898 he filed papers for the rights to the California, Jupiter, and Cornet claims. In 1899 he staked the Model Claim, filling out the papers in his German dialect: "Dis claim is situated about 12 miles northwest of de Buffalo Hump, better known as de Morgan Diggens."

In the spring of 1899, Arnold built a new cabin at the foot of Umbrella Butte on the trail between Florence and Buffalo Hump.

Shortly after 1900, Arnold left the Florence area and hooked up with Fred Burgdorf, a German immigrant who arrived in Warren in 1864, but who left the goldfields for a location then known as Warm Springs, a natural hot spring. It was located on the trail between Florence and Warren. He erected a hotel to lodge the miners, and he persuaded officials in

Washington, D.C., to establish a post office there named "Resort."

Some accounts say that Arnold actually found the hot springs before Burgdorf did. Others argue the two men found it together. Burgdorf clearly filed the claim to the place, and in 1902 it became his.

There seemed to be no hard feelings between the partners since Arnold remained at Resort for the next twenty years. In November of 1912, he ran for constable against George Looper. When they each received one vote, they shared the office.

In 1920 Arnold was a boarder living with Burgdorf at his resort. Over seventy, he still managed to work a few claims. In the late 1920s, he moved seventeen miles north to the Salmon River, where he formed a partnership with Lillian Standish, who lived across the river from French Creek. The two mined on Bear Creek, part of the Marshall Mountain District on the south side of the river. Standish had a comfortable home, and Arnold stayed there when he was not at the mines.

On February 3, 1933, at age eighty-three, Arnold suffered a stroke that left him paralyzed. He died seven days later at the Standish home. His obituary noted that he was a prominent miner of central Idaho, where he had lived for over fifty years. He was buried below a rocky bluff behind the Standish house. No marker survives at his gravesite, and its exact location is now lost.

Sylvester Scott

His nickname was "Bear," and Sylvester Scott used it with pride. His search for adventure and the need to provide for his family brought him to the Salmon River.

Sylvester Scott was born on May 16, 1837, in Darlington, Wisconsin, a ninth-generation American. Thomas Scott, Sylvester's first grandfather in America, arrived in Connecticut in November 1643.

Scott's father, Rotheus Hayward Scott, was born in Ohio. He married three times, outliving his first two wives. Sylvester's mother, Elizabeth Hamilton Scott, died shortly after he was born. He was her only child. Rotheus Scott eventually remarried; in all, he would have eleven children.

On September 23, 1853, Sylvester Scott married Malinda Miller. He was sixteen; she was only twelve. In the mid 1850s, the Scotts made the long journey to California to begin a new life. Accompanied by Rotheus and his wife, and Thomas Scott, Sylvester's oldest half-brother, they settled in Sonoma County, staking a 4,000-acre ranch where they planned to raise cattle. Bear and cougar raised havoc with their livestock, however, so instead they turned to hunting deer and bear.

In September 1859, Malinda delivered their first child, a son, Newton. Over the next twenty-six years, she had nine boys— Charles, Obediah, Riley, Ira, Lewis, Frank, Reuben, Walter, and Fred—and nine girls—Elizabeth, Rebecca, Delilah, Lucy, Ruth, Sarah, Dolly, Etta, and Prudence, all born in California.

While Malinda was raising the children, Sylvester was providing for them. The Scotts were proficient deer hunters;

Sylvester Scott's grave, located northwest of the cabin at the Scott Ranch, provides an excellent panorama of the French Creek drainage.

venison fed the family, and they sold the hides for $13 a dozen in San Francisco. Their hunting prowess, especially Sylvester's, was widely admired.

Sylvester bolstered his image by dressing the part. A large man with dark, deep-set eyes, black hair, and a full mustache, he often wore buckskin, a coonskin cap, and carried his Bowie knife tucked in his belt. As his reputation spread, people came to his ranch to participate in his hunts. The Prince of Wales, later Edward VII, was one such visitor. He was so impressed with Scott that he sent him a fine English rifle still cherished by the Scott family.

Sylvester's intimidating appearance complemented his no-

nonsense attitude. He was stern and demanding of his children, and they learned to tow the line. He was also very protective of his daughters, which some men discovered the hard way. Once Scott employed the butt of his English rifle on the head of a man intent on seducing one of them. In another instance, Sylvester killed a man with similar intentions.

California was good for the Scotts. Eventually, though, the game was depleted, and people increased. Sylvester was eager to find a better livelihood. In the early 1890s, he gathered most of his family and traveled northeast to Idaho, where they settled near present Cascade in what became known as Scott Valley. They planned to raise cattle and hunt, but the winter of 1893 was severe. By the time spring arrived, Scott had only one cow, two horses, and a wagon. Searching for more hospitable surroundings, he chose the Salmon River Canyon. He scouted the reach near Riggins and found a place across from French Creek, a mile northeast from the river on the trail to Florence. Family legend has it that he traded his two horses and his wagon for the property.

The rest of the family followed him to the river. They built a house and a barn, cleared the land, and put in an orchard and garden. With the help of Chinese workers, they dug an extensive irrigation system, using the water from Robbins Creek. Their labors provided food for themselves, and they sold the excess to the miners in Florence and Warren. The Scotts became well known in the area for their fairness and determination.

Scott also invested in mining, staking several claims

between Florence and the Salmon River. On July 15, 1897, he staked the King of the Salmon River claim, which became part of their homestead.

In 1897 Newton Scott, the oldest son, was killed by a falling tree on the trail from Slate Creek to Florence. He was buried in the Florence cemetery. Another son, Obediah, was accidentally shot and killed while working on a farm near Grangeville. The remaining children scattered across the west—some to Oregon, others returning to California. Reuben remained on the ranch and filed for a homestead on 160 acres. His patent was granted in June 1924.

Scott died at the ranch on August 22, 1903. He was buried northwest of his original house. The gravestone was placed by Beverly Eason, who inherited the Scott Ranch from her Uncle Reuben. Eason brought the stone to the ranch in the 1950s on the back of a Honda 90 trail bike. Sylvester Scott's grave lies just outside the boundaries of the Scott Ranch on Forest Service land.

Jonathon Hackett

Jonathon Wright Hackett lies buried in the shadows of the mountain ridges on Fall Creek, a tributary to the Salmon River which is a long way from his old Kentucky home.

Hackett was born in August 1844, in Jefferson, Kentucky. His father was from England, his mother from Ohio. He spent much of his early life in Kentucky, where he farmed with his father.

Jonathon Hacket is buried on the east side of French Creek Road, approximately six road miles south of the Salmon River. The grave is located on the east side of Fall Creek and east of the ruins of an old cabin.

On November 8, 1861, shortly after the start of the Civil War, Hackett enlisted in the Union Army at West Union, Ohio, with Company C, 70th Regiment, Ohio Volunteer Infantry. His enlistment papers describe him as light-haired, gray-eyed, five feet, ten inches tall. He was eighteen at the time.

A month after his enlistment, Private Hackett traveled with his regiment to Paducah, Kentucky, before marching into Tennessee where he came face to face with combat. He survived the Battle of Shiloh and the siege of Corinth, which together cost the Union forces 13,000 men. Then he was dispatched to Memphis, where preparations began for a march to Vicksburg, Mississippi. In May of 1862, he was hospitalized with erysipelas, a highly contagious streptococcus infection. Hackett returned to his unit in June, but in August he was back in the hospital. In early September 1862, he deserted and returned to his home in Kentucky. He was never charged, but he was also never discharged from the army.

Once in Kentucky, Hackett became a miller. In June 1878, he met and married Martha (Mattie) Haley in Lewisville, Kentucky. Together they had seven children; four survived to adulthood. Their oldest son, Herbert, led his parents to Idaho and the Salmon River.

Herbert Hackett arrived in Idaho around 1898, first in Warren, then on the Salmon River, and then up Fall Creek, where he established several claims. In 1903 Hackett bought the Fall Creek Mining Company. Jonathon, his father, arrived shortly thereafter to assist his son with his mining operations. Mattie may not have accompanied him; however, they were still married at the time of his death.

Father and son traveled the various mining districts of central Idaho. They filed many claims in the Marshall Lake and Florence Districts: Victor, Blue Grass, Snowbird, and Badger, to name a few.

Herbert married and raised a family at the Fall Creek site. He built a cabin and cared for his wife and children there, while he and his father improved their mining operations.

On May 10, 1910, they were working one of their claims.

Jonathon was repairing a wooden flume when the dam above him broke. Before he could escape, he was washed down the flume and drowned. He was buried on Fall Creek, just east of the family cabin.

Following Jonathon's death, Mattie, who was living in Clarkston, Washington, filed for veteran's benefits. Her request was denied because Jonathon was a deserter.

Herb Hackett and his family remained on Fall Creek until 1930. Family members returned to the area in 1933 and have visited the site periodically. Raeburn Hackett, who was born ten days before Jonathon's accident, made regular visits to his childhood home. He died in 1991 and is buried next to his grandfather.

John Kelly

John Kelly was afflicted with gold fever. From his youth to the final day of his life, he sought that fabulous lode. In the end, his quest cost him his life.

Kelly was born in Massachusetts in 1827 to American-born parents. His father was from New Hampshire, his mother from Massachusetts. Seeking his fortune, young Kelly traveled to California as a forty-niner. In 1850 he was in El Dorado County, working the placer claims of French Canyon. He earned four dollars a day.

When gold was discovered in Idaho in 1861, Kelly moved to the Florence District and began buying and selling claims. He bought his first claim, the Harmon and Black claim, in early September 1862, for $100. Over the next fifteen years, he staked thirteen more claims at Florence, predominantly in Humbug Gulch. He also had claims on French Creek and French Gulch and formed his own mining company, Kelly & Company.

During the boom at Florence, he acquired the nickname of "Poker Kelly." However, it only appears twice in the account of his life: in his obituary and on his tombstone.

Kelly's claims proved unsuccessful, and by 1880 his financial condition was marginal. Florence was finished. Hard winters—some miners reported as much as sixteen feet of snow on Main Street—drove many away. Surviving in Florence, where an egg cost a dollar and a bottle of mustard as much as five, made Kelly decide to leave as well. He moved down to the Salmon River near French Creek, where he found employment with Frederick Shearer, working as a servant for room and board. He had not given up hope of returning to his claims, however. In the 1880 federal census, although employed by Shearer, Kelly still stated his trade as "gold miner."

Kelly left Shearer's place to settle at the mouth of present Kelly Creek, one mile up river from Spring Bar Campground on the Salmon River. By 1889, Kelly had built a small cabin on the flat near the mouth of the creek. An elaborate flume brought water from the creek to his well-maintained garden. In addition, he returned to working several mining claims on Kelly Creek and in the nearby area known as "The Crevice." Kelly lived and worked here until his death in 1899.

Conflicting stories surround the circumstances of his death.

The grave of John Kelly is visible on the north side of the Salmon River Road, approximately three-quarters of a mile east of Spring Bar, eleven miles east of Riggins.

One says that friends found him dead in his cabin, sitting in his favorite wicker chair, his dinner still on the stove. He appeared to have suffered a head injury, and in examining the mine near his cabin, they found evidence of a cave-in. The men—Jack Howard, Louie Howard, and George Shearer—took lumber from Kelly's flume, built a coffin, and buried him 100 yards from his cabin.

Another story in *The Idaho County Free Press* on September

18, 1899, reported that the decomposed body of Kelly was found August 28, 1899, inside his mine. Those who found him stated that a large boulder had fallen from the roof of the mine and had broken his back. They buried his body near his cabin.

Kelly's cabin has long since disappeared; a faded wooden headboard marks his grave. The nearby creek and mountain bear his name.

John Seaberg

John Seaberg came to America from Sweden, looking not only for a new life but also for a new identity.

Discrepancies exist concerning Seaberg's early days in this country. He may have arrived in the United States as early as 1895, when he was twenty-five. Shortly thereafter, he moved to Idaho in order to mine, and in 1900 he lived near Burgdorf as a boarder with Frank Perkins. Census records reveal he worked as a miner but could neither read, write, or speak English. However, in the 1910 census, he listed his age as forty-three and declared he was a naturalized citizen who had arrived in America in 1899. He also stated that "Seaberg" was not his real name.

In 1903 Seaberg was living with his younger brother, Nelson Anderson, in a cabin three miles south of Florence. Nelson came to the United States in 1896. Together they placer mined in the Florence Basin. In June of 1903, John filed a claim on the Golden Gate Mine. The Venus, Gold Leaf, and

Miller stakes followed, filed by Nelson in May and June of 1904. The two brothers worked their claims, but none of them proved out. In September 1910, the brothers sold them for one dollar. In March 1911, Nelson died of tuberculosis, leaving John bereft.

Seaberg was known along the Salmon River and in Florence, but was also a bit reclusive. Because of his refined manners, some neighbors believed Seaberg once had been well off, but rumors circulated that bad investments had cost him his fortune. During the last years of his life, Seaberg was severely crippled, often unable to work. People on the river and in Florence looked after him.

Snowfalls in the Florence Basin were legendary. Although miners were known to exaggerate, during the grim winter of 1917-1918, the recorded snowfall was 37.8 feet. Since the promise of gold strikes in the basin had dwindled, by 1918 only the most resolute miners still worked the area, and few of them wintered there. Al DeFlong, a miner from Grangeville, had tried to persuade Seaberg to spend the winter with him in Grangeville, but Seaberg refused.

Like most miners, he had his share of difficulties. He smoked a pipe, and because of his arthritic hands, he kept a candle lit in his cabin at all times so he could easily restart his pipe. Late one night in early December 1918, Seaberg's cabin caught fire. It was visible for miles. When neighbors in the area finally arrived at the cabin, they found footprints leading to and from the cabin. Nearby was a pile of supplies, partially burned. Seaberg obviously had rescued some of his stores and then set off in the direction of Florence. Fresh snow

CHARLIE
(OR JOHN) SEABURG
DIED NOV. 1918
OF EXPOSURE
REMAINS FOUND
1931

The Florence cemetery, where Charlie Seaberg is buried, can be found by taking the Salmon River Road from Riggins nine miles to Allison Creek. At Allison Creek, take FS Road 221 and follow the signs approximately fifteen miles to Florence.

obscured his tracks, and although they searched for days, no other trace was found.

For thirteen years, Seaberg's disappearance remained a mystery. Then prospector Harvey Hillman discovered a skeleton about a mile from Florence. A match box with a peculiar type of match, a belt buckle, a patched pair of rubber boots, and a walking staff identified the remains as those of Seaberg.

When the *Idaho Country Free Press* reported the discovery,

the spelling of John's name changed to Sea*burg*. Other sources mention a Charlie Seaburg who was lost in the winter of 1918 in the Gospel-Hump area.

Hillman took the body to Florence and buried it in the Florence cemetery. Seaburg Point near Florence perpetuates the name he chose for himself.

William Allison

Allison Creek empties into the Salmon River nine miles east of Riggins on the Salmon River Road. From there, a one-time trail, now road, heads north following Allison Creek for six miles. The road meanders through the mountains to Florence and beyond. On this trail, William Allison staked his claim.

Allison was born in 1820 in Tennessee. His father came from New York; his mother was from Virginia. Little else is known about his origins.

Allison's year of arrival in Idaho is unknown as well, but records show he staked his claim on Allison Creek in early 1871. He built his cabin in a small valley on the creek, one mile from the creek's mouth on the Salmon. He did a little placer mining there, grew a large garden, and raised cattle. He provided meals and lodging for miners making their way to the Prospect Mine, three miles north, and eventually to Florence.

Allison kept to himself and never married. He seldom left his place. When he died on September 16, 1888, his obituary stated, "Mr. Allison of the Salmon River was found dead in his house on Sunday the 16th. Such deaths are pitiful. The living should learn that it is not right to isolate oneself from the neighbors."

Allison was buried on the west side of Allison Creek, just across the stream from his house. Although county officials searched for next of kin, they were unable to locate any. His property, which included horses, cattle, and personal belongings, was sold at public auction the following spring. Proceeds of the sale went to the county's general school fund.

Frank Riggins

Young boys fortunate enough to be raised on the Salmon River were taught early the skills necessary for survival in the rugged area. Hunting and fishing were a part of those skills and most boys, Frank Riggins included, jumped at the chance to show off their talents.

Frank was born December 11, 1900, to Fred and Clara Rowe Riggins. Shortly after his birth, his family moved to Hot Springs on the Salmon River, nine miles east of present-day Riggins. Fred bought the springs for $120. His goal was to farm and ranch, providing for his family by supplying the miners in Florence and Warren. At first it was difficult for the family. Frank, of course, was too young to realize it, but his early years were spent in a tent, while his parents labored to turn Hot Springs Bar into a successful business.

The waters attracted many visitors. Fred and Clara built a

The grave of Frank Riggins is located at the Salmon River Hot Springs Resort and is accessible only to guests. It is on the hillside, southwest of the main lodge.

seven-bedroom house to accommodate frequent guests. Additionally, they cared for their own children: Mildred, Alice, Frank, and Paul.

On July 12, 1911, Frank left the house around 9:00 a.m. to go hunting. He went alone, carrying his rifle. When he failed to return in the afternoon, the family went looking for him. They found him in a cornfield on the bar, his rifle beside him. It had accidentally discharged, killing him instantly.

He was buried on the hillside immediately behind the

house. The grave is marked by a small white stone surrounded by a white picket fence. Lilacs, planted around the grave by his family, now stand over ten feet tall.

John and Sarah Levander

Just north of Riggins and west up Race Creek, a small, shaded family cemetery occupies a flat in the Salmon River Canyon. John and Sarah Levander, respected Idaho pioneers, are buried there.

Sarah Cox Levander was from Gentry County, Missouri. She was born in 1850 and her family came west by wagon to the Oregon Territory, where they were early pioneers.

John Levander was born on December 27, 1837, in Sweden. In 1852 he came to the United States and joined a brother prospecting in California. At some point, John went east to Illinois, where he attended school and learned bookkeeping. In 1859 he bought a wagon and a yoke of oxen and drove west to Pikes Peak, Colorado.

Before long he went west again, ending up in the Willamette Valley in Oregon. He did odd jobs there, and once drove a herd of cattle to California. When Captain Pierce discovered gold in 1860 in the Clearwater Mountains, Levander followed the rush to Idaho. Soon after, he was in the goldfields of Boise Basin, where he ran a freight line and ranched.

John and Sarah's marriage, which took place in a tent, was the first to be formally recorded in the Boise Valley. They had seven children; five of them survived their parents.

In the ensuing years, John took care of his family and participated in early Idaho politics. He said he was Democrat and attended the first county convention held in Idaho (in Pierce). In 1882 he was the chairman of the Washington County Convention, and in 1884 he served a term as county commissioner.

The Levanders lived in the Meadows Valley area for several years, where John continued to ranch and haul freight for the mines. In December 1890, he carried $50,000 worth of gold from the Mayflower Mine near Warren to Weiser, Idaho.

In 1893, the Levanders sought the milder climate of the Salmon River and settled at the mouth of Race Creek, one mile north of present-day Riggins. On April 5, 1905, John filed for a homestead patent on 159 acres there. He and Sarah ran a way station, called Goff, serving miners bound for Florence, Warren, and Thunder Mountain. It consisted of a hotel, post office, mercantile, and feed store.

The hotel was among the finest buildings in the region: two stories, lace curtains, screened porch carpeted floors. Sarah's kitchen was equipped with running water from Race Creek. In 1905 son Homer installed a Pelton wheel on the creek and the family had electricity.

When Sarah's health began to fail and hotel upkeep became too demanding, they sold the business and built a new house, one-quarter mile up Race Creek. They were living there when Sarah died on May 29, 1909, of acute indigestion. She was fifty-eight. John buried her on a small flat behind their home. In December 1910, John sold the Race Creek

*John and Sarah
Levander share the
only headstone in the
Levander family
cemetery, located on
Race Creek Road,
one-quarter mile
west of Highway 95.*

property to Homer for $5,000. On February 26, 1914, after a
short illness, John Levander died. He was buried next to his
wife.

The hotel stood until 1979, when it burned in a spectacular
fire. The Levander house on Race Creek still stands, and the
family cemetery is located directly north of the house. Purple
irises bloom there every spring.

Richard Devine

An Englishman by birth, Richard Devine was a sailor who left the sea for a life of mining and ranching in the wilds of Idaho.

Devine arrived on the Salmon River as early as 1869. In July of that year, he sold his ranch and a mining claim, known as the Brown and Devine, to D. G. Shellenberger for $600 in gold.

He then moved to the mouth of Carver Creek, six miles north of present Riggins and built a small cabin located on a flat above the river. There he mined and raised cattle.

On the evening of June 13, 1877, Devine was alone when two young Nez Perce Indians, Red Moccasin Tops and Shore Crossing, burst into his cabin. Some accounts say Devine was shot when he opened the door; others report he was attacked, then shot with his own gun. In either event, he became the first white fatality of the Nez Perce War.

In the eyes of the Nez Perce, Devine's death was frontier justice. The Indians considered him ruthless, capable of any atrocity. Yellow Wolf, a Nez Perce Indian, said Devine cursed at the Indians and set his dogs on them when they passed his place. According to other sources, in 1876, after shooting and killing a crippled Indian named DaKoopin, Devine went unpunished.

White settlers along the river had a another viewpoint. When Devine arrived on the river, he brought along a fine English rifle, reputedly the best on the river. After his death, the rifle could not be found.

Devine was not the young Indians' victim of choice. They

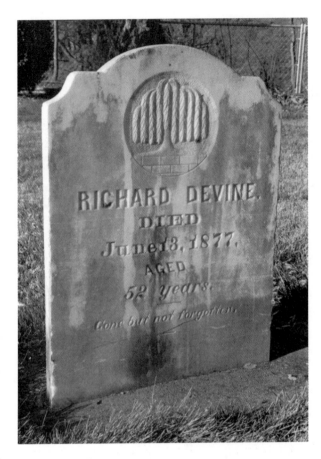

RICHARD DEVINE.
DIED
June 13, 1877.
AGED
52 years.
Gone but not forgotten.

The grave of Richard Devine is in the John Day cemetery, thirteen miles north of Riggins. The cemetery is situated one-quarter mile east of Highway 95, on a knoll that overlooks the Salmon River.

originally sought Larry Ott, a white man who lived at what was known as Horseshoe Bend, seven miles south of Whitebird. In the spring of 1874, Ott had killed Eagle Robe, chief of a Nez Perce band and father of Shore Crossing. After being taunted for not avenging his father's death, Shore Crossing set out to restore his honor. He went to confront Ott, but Ott was not home. Eager for a fight, the young braves settled for Devine.

Their retribution was the beginning of a three-month war.

Four days later, the Nez Perce and the U.S. Army fought the Battle of Whitebird. Red Moccasin Tops and Shore Crossing fought bravely. On August 9, 1877, both were killed at the Battle of the Big Hole in Montana.

Early reports state that Devine was buried near his cabin. His gravesite is now located at the John Day cemetery, eleven miles north of Riggins on John Day Creek. On a bluff that overlooks the Salmon River, it is one-quarter mile east of State Highway 95.

Following the war, Devine's property was sold for $510 to Amos Carver. Carver filed on the mining claim, and the creek there still bears his name.

Henry Elfers

Jurdin Henry Elfers, an adventurous spirit, left his homeland in Germany for the promise of America.

Elfers was born in 1834 in Hanover, Germany, the son of Burn and Adelaide Elfers. The opportunities in America drew him to the goldfields of California. Sailing around Cape Horn in 1849, he reached San Francisco and joined prospectors in search of the Mother Lode. He mined in California for over ten years. At some point, he teamed up with Harry Mason, another miner. When the two heard of gold strikes in Washington Territory, later Idaho, they came north, arriving first in Florence in 1862.

When Florence proved unprofitable, the partners drifted west to John Day Creek on the Salmon River. There they entered into a new partnership with John Wessel and started a ranch complete with a hotel, general store, sawmill, and stable. They also established a dairy with 200 cows and ran a pack train to supply the miners in Florence and Warren. They called their operation H. Mason & Company.

This partnership was dissolved April 1, 1865, when Elfers sold his share to Mason and Wessel for $1,000.

By 1870, Elfers was back in Germany, looking for a wife. He chose Catherine M. Beckroge, a twenty-five-year-old with a remarkable spirit. Elfers, Catherine, and Catherine's younger brother, Harry Beckroge, returned to the United States, disembarking in San Francisco in 1871. Catherine and Henry Elfers were married there on October 16.

They returned to Idaho, and Elfers looked up his old friend John Wessel. By this time, Wessel had bought out Mason and was sole owner of the John Day Ranch. In ill health, he was unable to take care of it by himself, so he again accepted Elfers as a partner. In his will, written in August 1872, Wessel divided his share of the ranch into thirds, leaving one to Elfers and the other two to his sisters, Anna and Maria. The will, however, stipulated that Elfers was to continue managing the property and, when he could afford it, he was to purchase Wessel's sisters' shares, leaving Elfers sole proprietor.

Wessel died the following February. Elfers took over the ranch and turned it into a thriving enterprise. His cattle and dairy businesses were profitable, and he and Catherine built a grand new hotel, which also served as their home. By June 1877, they had three children, with another on the way.

Elfers was well-liked by all who knew him. He was even

Henry Elfers, along with his wife and several of his children, is buried in the John Day cemetery, ground he once owned.

respected by the Nez Perce Indians. When a conflict arose between the Nez Perce and Harry Mason, they asked Elfers to serve on a council judging Mason's behavior toward them. It may have been Elfers' position on this council that led to his death.

On the night of June 13, when three young Indians stopped at the John Day Ranch, Elfers had no idea what prompted their visit. They told him they were looking for stray horses. None were found and the Nez Perce rode south upriver, where they killed Richard Devine.

Early the next morning, they returned to the Elfers' ranch, where they prepared an ambush. Elfers, Beckroge, and a hired hand named Richard Bland were moving cattle to a pasture located on a plateau above the house. Beckroge rode out first with the calves; Bland followed with the cows. Elfers brought up the rear with the stock horses. As each man rode up the path, the Indians picked them off. Then they entered Elfers' house and stole a rifle and some ammunition. At the time of the shootings, Catherine Elfers, two months pregnant, was in the milkhouse churning butter. She was completely unaware of the tragedy one-quarter mile away.

A river resident hunting in the area was alerted to the shooting by smoke from the Indians' rifles. When he went to investigate, he found the bodies of Elfers, Bland, and Beckroge on the trail. He went for help and returned with Norman Gould and George Greer. When Catherine was told, she refused to believe it. Only after the bodies were brought to the house did she accept the news.

Gould, a good friend of the Elfers' family, took Catherine and her children to Slate Creek. Two days later, Philip Cleary and several other men returned to the John Day Ranch and buried the three victims near a weeping willow tree by the ranch house.

Catherine Elfers remained at Slate Creek for six weeks before returning to the John Day Ranch. She directed that the bodies of her husband, brother, and Bland be moved to a small cemetery on a knoll overlooking the Salmon River, now known as the John Day cemetery. She hired Philip Cleary to manage the ranch. In January 1878, she gave birth to the Elfers' last child, Marie.

Cleary and Catherine eventually married, and Catherine remained on the ranch for many years to come. In February 1928, the John Day house built by Elfers burned.

Catherine died in May 1934 and is buried on the knoll between her first and second husbands.

Edward Robie

Edward Robie was an eighth-generation American, born June 20, 1834, in New York, to Jonathon and Sally Ladd Robie. The Robies were early colonists in New England, many of them settling in New Hampshire. Several members of the Robie family were soldiers in the Revolutionary War.

Not much is known about Edward's early life, except that he started west in the late 1850s. He was in Paris, Illinois, at the outbreak of the Civil War, and when the Union Army organized troops, he enlisted. On August 5, 1861, in St. Louis, he was assigned to Company B of Bissell's Missouri Engineer Regiment of the West.

Army life suited Robie, and he quickly rose through the ranks. By January 1862, he was a first sergeant. Soon, he made lieutenant. As a member of the engineer regiment, he rebuilt railroad lines damaged by the Confederates, constructed canals for U.S. gunboats, and cleared debris from the Mississippi River. He was at the siege of Vicksburg, Mississippi, and present at the surrender of Confederate

General John C. Pemberton.

After the fall of Vicksburg, army life began to wear on Robie. His regiment was ordered to Tennessee to repair railroad lines around Nashville and to construct a road from Nashville to the Tennessee River. On June 27, 1864, on a long march near Johnsonville, Tennessee, he was overcome by heat. His service record says he was treated for sunstroke at the regimental hospital from June 29 until July 20, after which he returned to duty.

Robie and his regiment were soon ordered to Georgia. On August 30 near Atlanta, when the troops neared Jonesboro, he again became ill. According to the assistant surgeon of his regiment, "said soldier was affected with sunstroke and gave out." Robie was hospitalized for fifteen days in September and then returned to his unit, now traveling with General Sherman on his march to the sea. Robie was in Savanah, Georgia, when it surrendered on December 22, 1864.

Four months later, the war was over and Lieutenant Robie was in Washington, D.C., for a grand review of the union troops. His regiment disbanded, and he was mustered out in Louisville, Kentucky, on July 22, 1865.

After his discharge he traveled west by way of Minnesota, arriving there sometime in 1868. Then he was on his way to Idaho, arriving with his mother and a brother in early 1872. Family records show he went first to Idaho City, then made his way to the Salmon River, working mining claims near Slate Creek, known then as Freedom.

Between 1872 and 1875, Robie, along with several partners, established a profitable mining operation in the goldfields near Florence. They employed Chinese miners, paying them fifty dollars a month. It was a good strike, and Robie reported earning as much as seventeen dollars an ounce.

In 1876 Robie left the river for Kamiah, Idaho, and worked for the federal government on the Nez Perce Indian Reservation for $1,000 a year. He supervised the gristmill, sawmill, and carpenter shops. At the time, he was one of only five white men living among the Indians there. In a letter written to a niece in January 1877, Robie explained that he

Ed Robie is buried on Russell Bar, twenty-four miles north of Riggins. The grave lies near a gravel pit and is protected by large rocks placed by Ron Mahurin, a grandson of Robie. (Earl Brockman photo)

had to "walk the Scratch while we are here to set an example for the Indians to follow." Six months later, however, Nez Perce warriors attacked and killed several settlers on the Salmon River, and the Nez Perce War began.

Robie was in Mount Idaho, near Grangeville, when the fighting commenced on June 13. He heard the stories of frightened survivors as they arrived. Isabella Benedict's story, in particular, caught his attention.

The Benedicts, together with their four children, lived near the mouth of Whitebird Creek. Samuel, the father, was one of the first victims of the war; Isabella, his wife, had escaped. When Robie learned this, he went looking for her. He found her and two of her daughters near the Johnson Ranch, eight miles southwest of Mount Idaho. He seated Isabella on his horse with one of the young girls, while he carried the other, and led them to the settlement.

Robie was commissioned as captain of the Grangeville Militia. The threat to the area was short-lived, however, and he saw no action against the Nez Perce.

Once the war was over, Robie returned to the Salmon River with a partner, Peter Smith. From 1878 to 1879, the two men paid $850 dollars in gold coin for all of the mining claims and property once owned by Jack Baker, a victim of the Nez Perce War. It occupied the east side of the river, four miles north of Slate Creek at Horseshoe Bend. Robie established his own residence on what is now known as Russell Bar.

On April 19, 1880, he married Isabella Benedict, and although he never formally adopted her four children, he raised them as his own. He and Isabella had four children of their own: Emily, Edward, Willie, and Alice.

Family life suited Robie. He developed the ranch and planted a variety of fruit trees. With Smith, he expanded his cattle and mining operations. One of the more successful ranchers on the river, he also made time for civic duties, serving as a trustee for the school district in 1888 and 1889. He was also an Idaho County commissioner.

On a stormy February 20, 1889, Robie left his home to attend a horse sale at Skookumchuck Creek, two miles downriver. He never returned. His body, partially covered with drifting snow, was found in the trail. He was buried two days later, next to his son Willie, who had died of smallpox a year earlier. Edward Robie was just fifty-four years old.

Isabella, now a widow for the second time, had seven children to feed. She immediately filed for a government pension, alleging Edward's early death was a result of the sunstroke he suffered during the war. She used affidavits from his commanding officers and a letter from Peter Smith to convince the War Department that Edward had never recovered. The War Department finally agreed and granted her a pension of $12 a month, which she received until her death in June 1911.

The homestead north of Slate Creek is still occupied by descendants of Edward and Isabella Robie.

William Osborn and Harry Mason

The lives of William Osborn and Harry Mason are joined by adventure, marriage, and tragedy.

No one buried on the Salmon River had a life so steeped in history as William Osborn, who was born on May 18, 1825, in Edgartown, Massachusetts. He was the son of Captain Samuel Osborn and Mary Cleveland Osborn, and a direct descendant of Elizabeth Tilley, who arrived in America on the Mayflower in 1620 with her parents, John and Joan Tilley. John and Joan Tilley died during the first winter in the New World, leaving thirteen-year-old Elizabeth an orphan. Shortly afterwards, she married John Howland, another Pilgrim. William Osborn was born seven generations later.

William's father was a master mariner with a fleet of ships recognized up and down the New England coast. He and his wife raised eight children; the boys, including William, were seafarers and whalers. At one time, Samuel Jr., William's brother, owned more whaling ships than anyone in the United States.

In the mid-1800s, the whaling business slowed; the family turned to hauling cargo along the seacoast from Maine to the Carolinas. But when a storm destroyed several ships in the Osborn fleet, William and his brother James decided it was time to try a new line of work. On September 13, 1849, they set sail on the ship *Splendid*, traveling south around Cape Horn to California. There they went to work in the goldfields with thousands of other young miners.

California did not match William's dreams. When he learned of new gold strikes in the mountains of Idaho, he

The grave of Henry Mason is located in the northeast corner of the French cemetery, surrounded by a pipe fence.

traveled north, arriving in Warren, Idaho Territory, sometime in 1864. James did not accompany him; in a poem, Caroline Osborn Reynolds writes that James died in a mining accident in California.

In Warren, Osborn was one of many working his claims. He was known for his resourcefulness and sense of humor, which he used to his advantage.

Catherine Eliza Klein, who also went by the name Elizabeth, and her sister Anna, were German immigrants who arrived in Boston in 1863. Seeking a better life, they sailed to San Francisco that fall. They remained in the city for two years. When Catherine learned of the promise of Idaho, the sisters traveled by ship to Lewiston, Idaho. From there, along with Anna and several other women, she rode the primitive trails on horseback to Warren.

When Osborn heard of the forthcoming arrival of the women, he took to the trail. With some of his friends, he strategically felled trees to block the way. When the women reached the log jam, William and his friends were there to lend a hand and, not incidentally, to obtain the first look at the women. William took an immediate liking to Catherine and she to him. Two years later, on October 29, 1867, they were married.

The couple remained in Warren for the next seven years. During that time they had four children: William, Caroline, Edward, and Anne. Then in 1874, William decided the family would be better off on the Salmon River. He and Catherine packed all of the family belongings and rode horseback to Remington Ferry, near present-day Whitebird. Little Willie rode with his father on his horse; Catherine followed on horseback, holding the baby Anne in her arms. The other two children were carried in baskets hung from a pack saddle.

The Osborns settled about two miles upstream from Whitebird Creek, on what was known as French Bar. William Osborn was an industrious provider and a good husband and father. He was well-liked by all the settlers along the river and the Nez Perce. On Saturday nights, he would take his turn bathing the children while Catherine read to him in her broken English.

Harry Mason, who had married Catherine's sister Anna, was already on the river when the Osborns arrived. Together Mason and Osborn worked placer claims on the bars along the river.

Mason was born in 1831, probably in Albany, New York. He was the son of Thomas Mason, a fur cutter, who had immigrated to the United States from England. In addition, Thomas had two other children, Tom and Helen.

Thomas Mason died in 1842. Harry did not see a future for himself in New York. Hearing of the riches in California, he decided to take a chance. In 1849 he shipped out on a whaler, sailing around Cape Horn and landing in San Francisco. For a time he continued as a sailor, working ships from San Francisco to the Sandwich Islands (present Hawaiian Islands). Eventually, however, he gave up the sea and settled in the goldfields of California. In 1860 he was living alone in Klamath County where he stated his net worth at $200.

In 1861 Mason joined Henry Elfers in a partnership that led them to Idaho. The two gathered supplies, put together a large pack train, and headed to Florence. It was not the bonanza they anticipated and after one year, they moved to the Salmon River and established a ranch on John Day Creek, thirty-three miles south of Grangeville. As mentioned earlier, John Wessel joined their partnership. The three of them built a substantial cattle operation and ran a pack train to supply the miners in Florence and Warren.

In 1865 Elfers sold his share and shortly thereafter, Mason's brother Tom arrived to assist with the ranch. However, in 1868 the Masons left for what is now known as Lewis County, where they established a stage station on the road from Lewiston to Mount Idaho. In time, the area became known as Mason Prairie.

By 1870 Harry had married Anna Klein. The Masons and their families worked the stage station until 1872, when Harry decided to return to the Salmon River. He and Anna purchased a ranch two miles south of Whitebird Creek. Harry opened a store there that served not only the settlers of the area but also the Nez Perce. In 1874 the Osborns joined him on the river, settling a half mile south.

In the spring of 1876, Anna Mason died and was buried on a hill overlooking the Salmon River near her home. Harry invited his sister and brother-in-law, Helen and Edward Walsh, to join him on the river. They accepted and Helen arrived on the river in the fall of 1876, accompanied by her two children, Edward and Masie. Her husband was to follow within a year.

In the spring of 1877, Mason had an altercation with two Nez Perce that led him to whip them. He faced an arbitration council but was cleared. Although he believed his actions had been justified, the Nez Perce thought differently.

On June 13, 1877, three young Indians stopped at Mason's store to examine a new Winchester rifle he had purchased. They wanted it and offered one of their horses in exchange. Mason refused and the Indians left. These young Indians then rode upriver and killed Richard Divine and Henry Elfers.

On the afternoon of June 14, Mason learned of the murders from William Osborn. Osborn was out helping neighbors harvest hay when a messenger arrived with news of the Nez Perce attack on John Day Creek. Mason initially dismissed the news as an isolated incident. When he learned Sam Benedict had been shot on Whitebird Creek, however, he took the news more seriously.

Mason sent word to his neighbors. Since it was the most defensible site in the area, he believed they should gather at his cabin. However, the other settlers had already decided to assemble at the Baker place, located at present-day Whitebird. William Osborn and Bill George, who worked with Osborn, gathered the Osborn family and rode toward Baker's house, stopping at Mason's on the way. Mason was reluctant to leave, but when Helen refused to go without him, he relented, and the group left together.

William Osborn is buried in the French cemetery on the east side of the old state highway, two miles south of Whitebird.

The two women, three men, and six children reached Baker's place at twilight. They crossed Whitebird Creek and approached, only to be accosted by several Nez Perce. They hid in the tall grass near Baker's cabin, and listened as the Indians called for a parley. Mason, who spoke for the group, refused, and the shooting began. George, who was shot in the hand, left the group and hurried to Mount Idaho.

Under darkness, the group retreated to Mason's cabin. Unable to follow the trail for fear of Indians, Mason and Osborn led the women and children up and down the steep hills and deep gulches that intersect the river in the Whitebird area. The younger children were carried in silence. Osborn's dog, which had followed the group, growled at every noise. To quiet him, Osborn had to cut its throat. The tattered group survived the night and arrived at Mason's the next morning. Surprisingly, they found Francois Chodoze, an employee of Mason's, and a man named Shoemaker fixing breakfast.

Determined to escape the Indians, Osborn and Mason decided to hide everyone across the river during the day and then recross the river at night and take the trail to Mount Idaho. They collected food and hurried to the boat landing, which was at Osborn's cabin. As soon as they reached the river, the Nez Perce appeared. The settlers, with the exception of Shoemaker, raced to the nearby cabin, barricaded the doors, and waited.

It is unclear what happened next. One report asserts that the Nez Perce asked the group to turn Mason over to them, and in exchange, they would let everyone else live. Another source states that Mason was the first to prepare to fire, but

Osborn asked him to stop. He wanted to negotiate with the Indians, with whom he was in good standing. In any event, the Nez Perce opened fire, shattering the only window in the cabin. The three men returned the fire, only to be struck by a second volley from the Indians. All three of them fell, Chodoze and Osborn mortally wounded.

Accounts of Osborn's last moments differ. One states that Osborn was killed immediately, shot through the heart. Another says he was knocked down in the first volley but survived to return fire before he was shot again. In yet a third version, Osborn was mortally wounded in the first exchange, but still managed to say to Catherine, "My God! Why did I ever bring you here?"

The women and children escaped the barrage of gunfire by hiding under one of the beds. Mason, whose right arm had been shattered by a bullet, hid beneath the other. The loss of blood made him delirious, and his sister could hear him muttering to himself, "twenty-seven, no, thirty-seven, no, forty-seven. That's it." He was forty-seven years old.

When no fire came from the cabin, the Indians stormed it. They chased the women and children out from under one bed, and they pulled Mason from beneath the other. In pain, he screamed, "Oh shoot me!" They did. Then the Nez Perce cast the bodies outside by the front door.

Some accounts state that the Indians then raped Catherine and Helen; the two women never confirmed the accusation. Catherine said the Indians ransacked the house and reported that only through the intervention of Chief Whitebird were she and her children spared.

The women brought blankets from the house and covered the bodies, using rocks to hold down the corners. Then they and the children walked to Slate Creek, where the Nez Perce assured them they would be safe.

Catherine and her four children reached Slate Creek and were taken in by John Woods. A week later, the dog Osborn had tried to silence arrived at the Woods' door. It had followed the family. The Osborns remained at Slate Creek for six weeks and then Catherine moved the family back to Warren, where she supported herself and the children by doing laundry. There she met Thomas Clay, whom she married in 1879. The family moved to Meadows Valley, where Catherine and her children lived out their days. Their descendants still call Meadows Valley home.

Helen Walsh was taken to Lewiston, where she reunited with her husband. Later she met with military officials to recount her story. She also wrote a detailed account of the events.

After the Battle of Whitebird, army troops were sent to bury the dead. Mason, Chodoze, and Osborn were buried in what is now known as the French cemetery. Osborne's original headstone, made of white marble and broken in half, tells of their ordeal. In part it reads "A devoted husband and dearly beloved father was torn from his happy family by the rude hands of savages. He has gone to a home where peace and happiness prevail."

Charlie Burlinghoff

Perhaps Charlie Burlinghoff was the only man in early Idaho killed in an argument over pigs.

Burlinghoff was born in 1863, likely in the Pacific Northwest. Early records confirm that he lived in the Palouse, having resided in Whitman and Latah counties.

On March 15, 1891, Burlinghoff married Lilly Evans, who was seventeen. They were married in Moscow, Idaho, and both stated they were residents of Latah County. Nine months later, on December 21, 1891, their first son, Jacob, was born.

In order to provide for his family, Burlinghoff worked as a farmhand around Moscow. He moved to Whitman County in 1893, where his second son Franklin was born in June. In 1895 Charlie packed up his family and moved to Whitebird. That year his only daughter, Lora, was born. In 1898 another son, Roy, was born. On his own, Burlinghoff purchased land and tried farming and raising cattle. He also frequented the local saloon.

On Sunday, February 11, 1900, Burlinghoff was in Whitebird sharing the afternoon with several other local residents. The conversation turned to an old lawsuit between Henry Ray and Troy Rogers over the ownership of some pigs. Ray, who was present, still harbored hard feelings toward Rogers over the outcome and insulted him. Burlinghoff was offended by Ray's insult directed at his friend, Rogers, and went after him with a bar stool. Ray drew a Colt .45 and shot Burlinghoff in the groin and in the shoulder. Soon afterwards, Burlinghoff died. Ray then surrendered to the justice of the peace, F. Z. Taylor.

Rather than calling the sheriff or coroner, Taylor convened a coroner's inquest and acted as coroner. He called witnesses from the saloon, and after listening to their testimony, he released Ray. His official report stated, "Charlie Burlinghoff came to his death by pistol wounds inflicted by the hand of Henry Ray in self-defense."

Burlinghoff was buried in the French cemetery near the Salmon River. His wife, seven months pregnant, could not afford a marker for his grave. In April, his child Lester was born. At the time of his death, Charlie owned two pieces of real property, four horses and a colt, and eighteen head of cattle. His debts totaled $276.

The four Burlinghoff boys, without a father, remained in Whitebird at the family farm, where they worked hard to support themselves and their mother. At the start of World War I, they registered for the draft. Of the four, Franklin was called to serve. He was shipped overseas and died in the trenches in France.

In 1927, Lilly Burlinghoff was visiting her daughter, Lora Niccols, in Star, Idaho. Lora had been having marital difficulties. Her husband had recently abandoned her, along with their eight children, and threatened to kill her. On May 4, he returned, but instead of shooting his wife, he shot and killed Lilly.

Lost Spirits Along the Salmon

It is impossible to document every burial on the Salmon. Many of them took place quickly, performed by people, sometimes strangers, who did their jobs and then quietly moved on. If a grave was marked, it was usually with a large stone or a cairn and over the years, it was forgotten.

In 1967 the Forest Service began marking some of the gravesites with wooden headboards. They were fastened to iron stakes set in concrete. Frances Zaunmiller Wisner, longtime resident of Campbell's Ferry, found the markers fitting. "They are simple markers," she said, "as the men were simple people."

Yet for all the marked graves, there may be hundreds that have been lost. Some were simply never marked; others were neglected and eventually lost. For them, we may never uncover their stories, so they truly remain the Spirits of the Salmon River. Seven such persons are included here.

Clarence Prescott—Born 1858 in Wisconsin, he died in 1921 in Kooskia. Some Forest Service records indicate Prescott was buried at the Whitewater Ranch next to his wife, Ella Churchill Prescott. One account states that he died at Newsome on the South Fork of the Clearwater and was buried there. Idaho death records say he died of exposure in Kooskia and was buried there. No record of him exists in the Kooskia cemetery.

William Whitmore (Whitworth)—Forest Service records indicate three burials near the mouth of Mackay Creek. One is William Mackay. According to Carrey and Conley, another belongs to Whitmore, who lived across the river from Mackay Bar. Census records indicate a William Whitworth living at that site in 1920. Whitworth was born in Oregon in 1860. No records of his death exist. Vern Wisner, longtime resident of Campbell's Ferry, reported to the Forest Service that the grave was that of Mackay's partner, W. S. Howenstine, who died sometime between 1910 and 1920.

Fred Ipe—Forest Service records indicate a young Indian boy is buried at the Mackay Bar cemetery. Carrey and Conley wrote that he committed suicide at the mouth of the South Fork. No other records are available.

William B. Knott—Knott earned a name for himself along the river as the proprietor of Knott's Ferry, which carried miners across the river on their way from Warren to Florence. Knott bought the ferry in November 1863 and sold it to Frank Shissler in June 1865. Knott moved from there to the Owyhee Mountains. Forest Service records say a grave at the old Ferry site may be that of Knott. Since Knott had left the area by 1880, it seems unlikely. The grave the Forest Service records is probably that of William Soards who was buried in the vicinity. No mention of Knott's death could be found in any Idaho County records.

Henry Beckroge—Brother-in-law of Henry Jurdin Elfers, Beckroge was killed along with Elfers in the first days of the Nez Perce War. It is unclear whether his name was Harry, Burn, or Henry. Supposedly, he was called "Harry" after an older brother, who died in Idaho before 1877, but no public record can be located. The younger Harry arrived in the United States in 1871, along with his sister Catherine, who then married Elfers. A headstone in the John Day cemetery reads Henry Beckrodge. He was 21 at the time of his death.

Francois Chodoze and August Bacon—Both of these men were killed in the Nez Perce War. Chodoze is often called "French Frank" in accounts of the war. He was with William Osborn and Harry Mason when they were killed. Most likely, he is buried in the French Cemetery along with other victims of the war. August Bacon probably also rests in the French cemetery. He was shot trying to protect the Benedict family. Isabella Benedict saw him killed when the Nez Perce attacked her home. Other than that they were French miners working the banks of the Salmon River, there is no record of Chodoze or Bacon.

Bibliography

Anglen, Carol Sams. *1886-1903 Idaho County Newspaper Vitals.* Orem, Utah: Ancestry, Inc. 1999.

Arrington, Leonard J. *History of Idaho, Vol. 1.* Moscow, Idaho: University of Idaho Press, 1994.

Bailey, Robert G. *The River of No Return.* 1947. Lewiston, Idaho: Lewiston Printing, 1983.

Brown, Mark H. *The Flight of the Nez Perce.* New York: Putnam and Sons, 1967.

Carrey, Johnny and Cort Conley. *The Middle Fork, A Guide.* Cambridge, Idaho: Backeddy Books, 1992.

———. *The River of No Return.* Cambridge, Idaho: Backeddy Books, 1978.

Catholic Church Records of the Pacific Northwest, Salem Register 1864-1885. Portland: Binford & Mort Publishing, 1992.

Centennial History of Lemhi County, Idaho. Volumes 1-3. Lemhi County Historical Committee, 1992.

Chedsey, Zona and Carolyn Frei, editors. *Idaho County Voices.* Grangeville: Idaho County Centennial Committee, 1990.

Conley, Cort. *Idaho Loners.* Cambridge, Idaho: Backeddy Books, 1994.

Dill, Lucy. American Local History Network—Idaho. "Killing on the Salmon River." 13 November 1999. http://www.usgennet.org/~alhnidus/idaho/rucker.html. 3 February 2000.

Elsensohn, Sister M. Alfreda. *Idaho County's Most Romantic Character: Polly Bemis.* Cottonwood, Idaho: Idaho Corporation of Benedictine Sisters, 1979.

————. *Pioneer Days in Idaho County.* Volumes I and II. Caldwell, Idaho: Caxton Printers, LTD, 1947.

Filer, Marybelle. "Historic Shepp Ranch Now Hunters' and Fishermen's Mecca." *Idaho County Free Press* [Grangeville] 16 June 1966.

Furey-Werhan, Carol. *Haven in the Wilderness.* Park, Arizona: Never Summer Ranch Publications, 1996.

Helmers, Cheryl. *Warren Times: a collection of news about Warren, Idaho.* Odessa, Texas, 1988.

Hough, Franklin B. *History of Lewis County, New York.* Syracuse, New York: D. Mason & Company, 1883.

Idaho Territorial Voters Poll List, 1863. Transcribed and edited by Gene Williams, 1996. Located at Idaho State Historical Library and Archives, Boise, Idaho.

Illustrated History of North Idaho. San Francisco/Spokane: Western Historical Publishing Company, 1903.

Lee, C. Robert. "My Family was Falling Apart." *Cosmopolitan.* September, 1959: 66-71.

Mann, Walter G. *Residents of the Salmon Rivers 1910 to 1920.* Payette National Forest.

————. "Wild Man Rucker." Unpublished Manuscript. Payette National Forest Heritage Program, 1969.

Manser, Eunice Clay and Murrielle McGaffee Wilson. *Riggins on the Salmon River.* Weiser, Idaho: Signal-American Printers, 1983.

McDermott, John D. *Forlorn Hope.* Boise: Idaho State Historical Society, 1978.

McWhorter, Lucullus Virgil. *Yellow Wolf: His Own Story.* Caldwell, Idaho: Caxton Printers, 1948.

Peterson, Harold. *The Last of the Mountain Men*. New York: Tower Books, 1969.

Povey, Dorothy. *Mining Camps of Idaho*. 1984.

Randolph, Julia I. *This Quiet Ground*. Bend, Oregon: Maverick Publications, 1989.

Records of the Proceedings of the District Court of Lemhi County. Roll 10, #3. Idaho State Library and Archives. Boise, Idaho.

Reddy, Sheila D. *The Color of Deep Water: The Story of Polly Bemis*. Payette National Forest, 1994.

————. *Wilderness of the Heart*. Payette National Forest, 1995.

Schumaker, O. Frank and James E. Dewey. *A History of the Salmon River Breaks Primitive Area*. U.S. Forest Service, 1970.

Shepp, Charles W. Unpublished diaries, 1902-1937. University of Idaho Special Collections. Smith, Elizabeth. *A History of the Salmon National Forest*. Ogden, Utah: United States Forest Service, 1970.

Walsh, Helen Julia Mason. "Personal Exieriences of the Nez Perce War." Unpublished manuscript. University of Washington Library, Seattle. A copy is also located at the Idaho State Historical Library and Archives, Boise, Idaho.

Wegars, Priscilla. "Charlie Bemis: Idaho's Most 'Significant Other'." *Idaho Yesterdays*. 44/3:3-17.

Wisner, Frances Zaunmiller. *My Mountains Where the River Still Runs Downhill*. Grangeville, Idaho: Idaho County Free Press, 1987.

Newspapers

Adams County Leader. Council, Idaho. Dec. 19, 1936.

The Buhl Herald. Twin Falls, Idaho. Sept. 7, 1933.

Elk City Mining News. Elk City, Idaho. Dec. 31, 1904

The Florence Miner. Florence, Idaho. January 8, 1898.

Idaho County Free Press. Grangeville, Idaho.

Aug. 9, 1934	Aug. 16, 1995	Oct. 9, 1958
Oct. 16, 1958	May 15, 1919	May 8, 1919
Sept. 18, 1919	May 22, 1919	July 23, 1931
Dec. 26, 1918	Feb. 23, 1933	Oct. 26, 1905
Oct. 27, 1921	June 13, 1935	May 12, 1932
Nov. 21, 1929	Oct. 13, 1932	Oct. 20, 1932
Dec. 13, 1928	Jan. 17, 1929	Dec. 12, 1929
Sept. 3, 1936	Aug. 11, 1932	Sept. 29, 1932
May 8, 1930	Sept. 15, 1932	Oct. 27, 1932
Aug. 5, 1926	Aug. 12, 1926	Mar. 11, 1909
Mar. 25, 1920	Aug. 2, 1945	Dec. 24, 1936
June 3, 1987	Feb. 11, 1898	Mar 26, 1898
Dec. 7, 1911	Dec. 21, 1911	Jan. 4, 1911
May 4, 1912	May 3, 1889	Oct. 24, 1890
June 3, 1987	Nov. 9, 1933	Oct. 5, 1933
Aug. 23, 1923		

The Idaho Recorder. Salmon, Idaho. Sept. 24, 1887.

The Idaho Statesman. Boise, Idaho

June 16, 1980	Mar. 17, 1960	Oct. 20, 1963
Aug. 8, 1971	May 1, 1980	July 9, 1998
June 5, 1987		

The Lemhi Herald. Salmon, Idaho.

May 13, 1909	Jan. 14, 1904	Feb. 2, 1904
Mar. 8, 1904	Aug. 25, 1904	Sept. 22, 1904

Oct. 16, 1904	Dec. 22, 1904	Mar. 23, 1905
March 4, 1909	Mar. 12, 1902	Feb. 25, 1909
April 22, 1909	April 29, 1909	May 6, 1909
Feb. 11, 1904	Oct. 22, 1903	Nov. 5, 1903
Nov. 19, 1903	Dec. 10, 1903	April 13, 1905
May 22, 1905	Nov. 2, 1905	Nov. 23, 1905
Feb. 16, 1906	Mar. 8, 1906	Feb. 23, 1906
April 26, 1906	June 7, 1906	Jan. 7, 1907

The Lewiston Morning Tribune. Lewiston, Idaho

Oct. 13, 1958	Oct. 15, 1958	Oct. 10, 1958
Oct . 11, 1958	May 1, 1980	

The Lewiston Teller. Lewiston, Idaho.

Aug. 22, 1878	Sept. 4, 1879	Aug. 29, 1879
Oct. 2, 1890	Sept. 25, 1890	

The Meadows Eagle. Meadow Valley, Idaho. 1911.

The Recorder Herald. Salmon, Idaho.

Nov. 24, 1943	Aug. 8, 1934	Aug. 15, 1935

Census Records

The following records were found at the Idaho State Historical Library and Archives in Boise.

California: 1850, 1860, 1870, 1880, 1900

Idaho: 1870, 1880, 1900, 1910, 1920

Iowa: 1870

Kentucky: 1880, 1890 Veteran's Schedule, 1900

Minnesota: 1900

Montana: 1880

New York: 1830, 1840, 1860

Nevada: 1870

Ohio: 1820, 1830

Oregon: 1870, 1880, 1895 (Marion County), 1900, 1920

Pennsylvania: 1870, 1880

South Dakota: 1890 Veteran's Schedule

Utah: 1920

Washington: 1880, 1900

Wyoming: 1880, 1900, 1910, 1920

Acknowledgments

This work would have been impossible without the help of the following, whose insight and knowledge of the Salmon River and its people were invaluable.

Ace Barton
Larry Kingsbury, Payette National Forest
Sister Catherine, St. Gertrude's Monestary
Ron Mahurin
The Records Department of Idaho County
The staff at the Idaho Historical Library and Archives
John Wolfe
George Russell
Rocky Wilson
Norm and Joyce Close
Dan Cook
Robin McRae
Bonnie Lym
Jack Standish
Cort Conley
Neil Sanders
Bessie Santos
Dolly Gill
Steve Matz, Salmon National Forest
Bernice Donaghue
Peter Filer
Knute at Yellow Pine Bar
Patti Burns, Lemhi County Auditor's Office
Peter Preston
Charlotte Armacost
Lucy Dill
Keith Darling

Index